WITHDRAWN

ISSUES THAT CONCERN YOU

Climate Change

Arthur Gillard, *Book Editor*

GREENHAVEN PRESS
A part of Gale, Cengage Learning

GALE
CENGAGE Learning™

Detroit • New York • San Francisco • New Haven, Conn • Waterville, Maine • London

Christine Nasso, *Publisher*
Elizabeth Des Chenes, *Managing Editor*

Articles in Greenhaven Press anthologies are often edited for length to meet page requirements. In addition, original titles of these works are changed to clearly present the main thesis and to explicitly indicate the author's opinion. Every effort is made to ensure that Greenhaven Press accurately reflects the original intent of the authors. Every effort has been made to trace the owners of copyrighted material.

Cover image copyright © David Shaw/Alamy

LIBRARY OF CONGRESS CATALOGING-IN-PUBLICATION DATA

Climate change / Arthur Gillard, book editor.
  p. cm. -- (Issues that concern you)
Includes bibliographical references and index.
ISBN 978-0-7377-5205-2 (hardcover)
1. Climatic changes--Social aspects. 2. Global warming--Social aspects.
3. Nature--Effect of human beings on. I. Gillard, Arthur.
QC903.C554 2011
363.738'74--dc22

2010036735

Printed in the United States of America
1 2 3 4 5 6 7 14 13 12 11

CONTENTS

Climate change may be the greatest challenge humanity has ever faced. While there are other dire threats to human existence—the risk of annihilation through nuclear war, for example, or the possibility of extinction through an asteroid colliding with the earth—for the first time humanity is faced with the serious possibility that the cumulative actions of billions of people simply going about their daily lives could so change the earth's biosphere that civilization or even the very survival of the species might be threatened.

An indication of the disruptive effects human activity can have on the earth's biosphere came in the 1980s, when chlorofluorocarbons (CFCs) in such items as aerosol cans and refrigerators were determined to be causing massive damage to the ozone layer that protects all life on earth from the harmful effects of solar and cosmic radiation. It was revealed that if the world had continued to use CFCs, the damage to the ozone layer would have continued to get worse, with increasingly dire consequences. By banning the use of CFCs, an environmental catastrophe was averted, and while this shows the potential for civilization to recognize and deal with a global climate crisis, it may also indicate, as science journalist Dianne Dumanoski puts it, that the world had entered "a new and ominous epoch when human activity began to disrupt the essential but invisible planetary systems that sustain a dynamic, living Earth."[1]

As far back as the late nineteenth century, it was suspected that the accumulation of greenhouse gases in the earth's atmosphere since the beginning of the Industrial Revolution might cause the planet to heat up. Swedish chemist Svante Arrhenius first suggested the possibility in 1896. Since then a growing amount of scientific investigation has steadily confirmed the plausibility of this scenario. Toward the end of the twentieth century the investigation became more systematic, with entire organizations devoting time to studying the problem. In 1988 the United Nations formed the

Intergovernmental Panel on Climate Change (IPCC) to evaluate, synthesize, and report on the most reliable scientific research and opinion regarding the issue. Since the IPCC issued its first report in 1990, the warnings of possible climate change scenarios have become increasingly serious. Yet much of the real-world data on climate change has been faster and more extreme than the worst scenarios in its reports, leading an increasing number of scientists to speculate that the world may be approaching some sort of climatic

No matter what side of the climate change issue one stands on, the two factions are able to agree on one issue: that there is only one planet.

"tipping point" beyond which sudden and irreversible changes may happen no matter what action is taken. Richard Alley of Penn State University warned in 2002 that "the more the climate is forced to change, the more likely it is to hit some unforeseen threshold that can trigger quite fast, surprising and perhaps unpleasant changes."[2] As climate researcher Wally Broeker puts it, "Climate is an angry beast, and we are poking it with sticks."[3]

Indeed, as scientists have become more adept at determining how the climate had changed in the past, they have been able to verify that the earth's climate can change extremely rapidly, even under natural conditions. As Greg Craven notes in *What's the Worst That Could Happen? A Rational Response to the Climate Change Debate*, "Researchers . . . now have good evidence that 14,000 years ago, Greenland warmed up by 20 degrees Fahrenheit in just 50 years, with a change of up to 5 degrees from one year to the next, and a reorganization of atmospheric circulation in just 1 to 3 years."[4]

While scientific consensus verifying climate change has been growing, the issue in the popular media has been mixed, with a bewildering array of perspectives on all sides, making it very difficult for nonscientists to make sense of it all or decide what needs to be done about it.

But while there is still a vocal minority of people who claim either that climate change is not happening or that it is entirely a natural phenomenon, many would now agree with President Barack Obama, who in 2006 said that

All across the world, in every kind of environment and region known to man, increasingly dangerous weather patterns and devastating storms are abruptly putting an end to the long-running debate over whether or not climate change is real. Not only is it real, it's here, and its effects are giving rise to a frighteningly new global phenomenon: the man-made natural disaster.[5]

Increasingly the debate is not so much over whether climate change is really happening, or whether human activity is significantly contributing to it, but revolves around questions about the magnitude of the crisis, how much time is left to solve it, what should be done to avert catastrophe, whether it is already too late, and how much effort should be put into preventing climate change versus adapting to the changing climate.

Authors in this anthology offer a variety of perspectives on climate change. In addition, the volume contains several appendices to help the reader understand and explore the topic, including a thorough bibliography and a list of organizations to contact for further information. The appendix titled "What You Should Know About Climate Change" offers facts about this topic. The appendix titled "What You Should Do About Climate Change" offers advice for young people who are concerned with the issue. With all these features, *Issues That Concern You: Climate Change* provides an excellent resource for everyone interested in this crucial topic.

Notes

1. Edward Wolf, "Straight Talk for the Planetary Era: A Trio of Book Reviews," November 17, 2009. www.worldchanging.com/archives/010701.html.

2. Richard Alley, "Quotes: Climate Change," *New Scientist*, September 4, 2006. www.newscientist.com/article/dn9910-quotes-climate-change.html.

3. Greg Craven, *What's the Worst That Could Happen? A Rational Response to the Climate Change Debate.* New York: Penguin, 2009, p. 175.

4. Craven, *What's the Worst That Could Happen?* p. 174.

5. Barack Obama, "Energy Independence and the Safety of Our Planet," April 3, 2006. http://obamaspeeches.com/060-Energy-Independence-and-the-Safety-of-Our-Planet-Obama-Speech.htm.

ONE

The Impact of Climate Change on the United States

U.S. Global Change Research Program

The U.S. Global Change Research Program (USGCRP) coordinates and integrates federal research on changes in the global environment and their implications for society. Since its founding in 1989, the USGCRP has made the world's largest scientific investment in the areas of climate change and global change research, supporting research and observation in collaboration with several other national and international science programs. The following viewpoint summarizes the results of a report published in 2009 by the U.S. Global Change Research Program on climate change impacts in the United States. According to the report, changes in climate have already been observed both in the United States and around the world and are caused mainly by heat-trapping gases produced by human activity. The authors note that there is uncertainty in predicting future scenarios, but they claim that large, unpredictable and severe climate changes are likely by the middle of the twenty-first century. The report states that the two approaches humanity can take are either to adapt to the effects of climate change or to mitigate those effects by reducing the amount of heat-trapping gases released into the atmosphere.

Global Climate Change Impacts in the United States: A State of Knowledge Report from the U.S. Global Change Research Program. New York: Cambridge University Press, 2009. Reprinted with the permission of Cambridge University Press.

Observations show that warming of the climate is unequivocal. The global warming observed over the past 50 years is due primarily to human-induced emissions of heat-trapping gases. These emissions come mainly from the burning of fossil fuels (coal, oil, and gas), with additional contributions from the clearing of forests and agricultural activities.

Warming Will Increase Considerably This Century

Warming over this century is projected to be considerably greater than over the last century. The global average temperature since 1900 has risen by about 1.5°F [1.5 degrees Fahrenheit]. By 2100, it is projected to rise another 2 to 10°F. The U.S. average temperature has risen by a comparable amount and is very likely to rise more than the global average over this century, with some variation from place to place. Several factors will determine future temperature increases. Increases at the lower end of this range are more likely if global heat-trapping gas emissions are cut substantially. If emissions continue to rise at or near current rates, temperature increases are more likely to be near the upper end of the range. Volcanic eruptions or other natural variations could temporarily counteract some of the human-induced warming, slowing the rise in global temperature, but these effects would only last a few years.

Reducing emissions of carbon dioxide would lessen warming over this century and beyond. Sizable early cuts in emissions would significantly reduce the pace and the overall amount of climate change. Earlier cuts in emissions would have a greater effect in reducing climate change than comparable reductions made later. In addition, reducing emissions of some shorter-lived heat-trapping gases, such as methane, and some types of particles, such as soot, would begin to reduce warming within weeks to decades.

Changes Have Already Been Observed

Climate-related changes have already been observed globally and in the United States. These include increases in air and water temperatures, reduced frost days, increased frequency and intensity of heavy downpours, a rise in sea level, and reduced snow cover, glaciers, permafrost, and sea ice. A longer ice-free period on lakes and rivers, lengthening of the growing season, and increased water vapor in the atmosphere have also been observed. Over the past 30 years, temperatures have risen faster in winter than in any

Photos of Glacier National Park's shrinking Grinnell Glacier taken in 1940 (top) and 2004 may show the effects of global warming.

other season, with average winter temperatures in the Midwest and northern Great Plains increasing more than 7°F. Some of the changes have been faster than previous assessments had suggested.

These climate-related changes are expected to continue while new ones develop. Likely future changes for the United States and surrounding coastal waters include more intense hurricanes with related increases in wind, rain, and storm surges (but not necessarily an increase in the number of these storms that make land-fall), as well as drier conditions in the Southwest and Caribbean. These changes will affect human health, water supply, agriculture, coastal areas, and many other aspects of society and the natural environment. . . .

Changes Will Be Severe and Unpredictable

Society and ecosystems can adjust to some climatic changes, but this takes time. The projected rapid rate and large amount of climate change over this century will challenge the ability of society and natural systems to adapt. For example, it is difficult and expensive to alter or replace infrastructure designed to last for decades (such as buildings, bridges, roads, airports, reservoirs, and ports) in response to continuous and/or abrupt climate change.

Impacts are expected to become increasingly severe for more people and places as the amount of warming increases. Rapid rates of warming would lead to particularly large impacts on natural ecosystems and the benefits they provide to humanity. Some of the impacts of climate change will be irreversible, such as species extinctions and coastal land lost to rising seas.

Unanticipated impacts of increasing carbon dioxide and climate change have already occurred and more are possible in the future. For example, it has recently been observed that the increase in atmospheric carbon dioxide concentration is causing an increase in ocean acidity. This reduces the ability of corals and other sea life to build shells and skeletons out of calcium carbonate. Additional impacts in the future might stem from unforeseen changes in the climate system, such as major alterations in oceans, ice, or storms; and unexpected consequences of ecological changes, such as massive dislocations of species or pest outbreaks. Unexpected social or economic changes, including major shifts in wealth, technology, or societal priorities would also affect our ability to respond to climate change. Both anticipated and unanticipated impacts become more challenging with increased warming. . . .

In projecting future conditions, there is always some level of uncertainty. For example, there is a high degree of confidence in projections that future temperature increases will be greatest in the Arctic and in the middle of continents. For precipitation, there is high confidence in projections of continued increases in the Arctic and sub-Arctic (including Alaska) and decreases in the regions just outside the tropics, but the precise location of the transition between these is less certain. At local to regional scales and on time frames up to a few years, natural climate variations can be relatively large and can temporarily mask the progressive nature of global climate change. However, the science of making skillful projections at these scales has progressed considerably, allowing useful information to be drawn from regional climate studies. . . .

How to Deal with Climate Change

This report focuses on observed and projected climate change and its impacts on the United States. However, a discussion of these issues would be incomplete without mentioning some of the actions society can take to respond to the climate challenge. The two major categories are "mitigation" and "adaptation." Mitigation refers to options for reducing heat-trapping emissions such as carbon dioxide, methane, nitrous oxide, and halocarbons, or removing some of the heat-trapping gases from the atmosphere. Adaptation refers to changes made to better respond to present or future climatic and other environmental conditions, thereby reducing harm or taking advantage of opportunity. Effective mitigation measures reduce the need for adaptation. Mitigation and adaptation are both essential parts of a comprehensive climate change response strategy.

Carbon dioxide emissions are a primary focus of mitigation strategies. These include improving energy efficiency, using energy

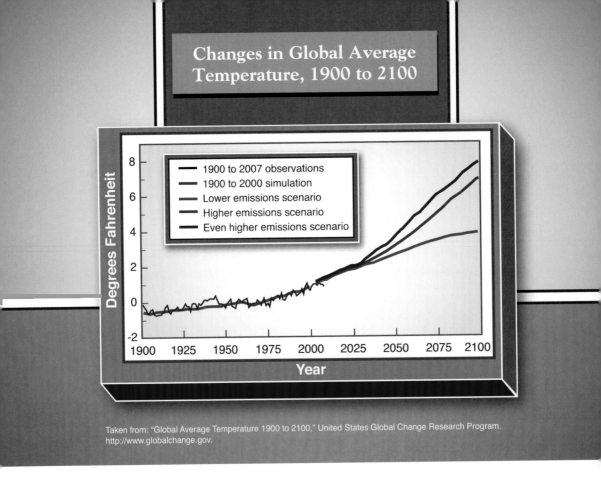

Changes in Global Average Temperature, 1900 to 2100

Degrees Fahrenheit

- 1900 to 2007 observations
- 1900 to 2000 simulation
- Lower emissions scenario
- Higher emissions scenario
- Even higher emissions scenario

Year

Taken from: "Global Average Temperature 1900 to 2100," United States Global Change Research Program. http://www.globalchange.gov.

sources that do not produce carbon dioxide or produce less of it, capturing and storing carbon dioxide from fossil fuel use, and so on. Choices made about emissions reductions now and over the next few decades will have far-reaching consequences for climate-change impacts. The importance of mitigation is clear in comparisons of impacts resulting from higher versus lower emissions scenarios considered in this report. Over the long term, lower emissions will lessen both the magnitude of climate-change impacts and the rate at which they appear. Smaller climate changes that come more slowly make the adaptation challenge more tractable.

Adapting to Climate Change

However, no matter how aggressively heat-trapping emissions are reduced, some amount of climate change and resulting impacts will continue due to the effects of gases that have already been released. This is true for several reasons. First, some of these gases are very long-lived and the levels of atmospheric heat-trapping gases will remain elevated for hundreds of years or more. Second, the Earth's vast oceans have absorbed much of the heat added to the climate system due to the increase in heat-trapping gases, and will retain that heat for many decades. In addition, the factors that determine emissions, such as energy-supply systems, cannot be changed overnight. Consequently, there is also a need for adaptation.

Adaptation can include a wide range of activities. Examples include a farmer switching to growing a different crop variety better suited to warmer or drier conditions; a company relocating key business centers away from coastal areas vulnerable to sea-level rise and hurricanes; and a community altering its zoning and building codes to place fewer structures in harm's way and making buildings less vulnerable to damage from floods, fires, and other extreme events. . . . However, it is clear that there are limits to how much adaptation can achieve.

Humans have adapted to changing conditions in the past, but in the future, adaptations will be particularly challenging because society won't be adapting to a new steady state but rather to a moving target. Climate will be continually changing, moving at a relatively rapid rate, outside the range to which society has adapted in the past. The precise amounts and timing of these changes will not be known with certainty.

Climate Change in Other Nations Affects the United States

In an increasingly interdependent world, U.S. vulnerability to climate change is linked to the fates of other nations. For example, conflicts or mass migrations of people resulting from food scarcity and other resource limits, health impacts, or environmental stresses in other parts of the world could threaten U.S. national security. It is thus difficult to fully evaluate the impacts of climate change on the United States without considering the consequences of climate change elsewhere.

What to Expect over the Next Century

1. *Global warming is unequivocal and primarily human-induced.*
Global temperature has increased over the past 50 years. This observed increase is due primarily to human-induced emissions of heat-trapping gases.

2. *Climate changes are underway in the United States and are projected to grow.*
Climate-related changes are already observed in the United States and its coastal waters. These include increases in heavy downpours, rising temperature and sea level, rapidly retreating glaciers, thawing permafrost, lengthening growing seasons, lengthening ice-free seasons in the ocean and on lakes and rivers, earlier snowmelt, and alterations in river flows. These changes are projected to grow.

3. *Widespread climate-related impacts are occurring now and are expected to increase.*
Climate changes are already affecting water, energy, transportation, agriculture, ecosystems, and health. These impacts are different from region to region and will grow under projected climate change.

4. *Climate change will stress water resources.*
Water is an issue in every region, but the nature of the potential impacts varies. Drought, related to reduced precipitation, increased evaporation, and increased water loss from plants, is an important issue in many regions, especially in the West. Floods and water quality problems are likely to be amplified by climate change in most regions. Declines in mountain snowpack are important in the West and Alaska where snowpack provides vital natural water storage.

5. *Crop and livestock production will be increasingly challenged.*
Agriculture is considered one of the sectors most adaptable to changes in climate. However, increased heat, pests, water stress, diseases, and weather extremes will pose adaptation challenges for crop and livestock production.

6. *Coastal areas are at increasing risk from sea-level rise and storm surge.*

Sea-level rise and storm surge place many U.S. coastal areas at increasing risk of erosion and flooding, especially along the Atlantic and Gulf Coasts, Pacific Islands, and parts of Alaska. Energy and transportation infrastructure and other property in coastal areas are very likely to be adversely affected.

7. *Threats to human health will increase.*

Health impacts of climate change are related to heat stress, waterborne diseases, poor air quality, extreme weather events, and diseases transmitted by insects and rodents. Robust public health infrastructure can reduce the potential for negative impacts.

8. *Climate change will interact with many social and environmental stresses.*

Climate change will combine with pollution, population growth, overuse of resources, urbanization, and other social, economic, and environmental stresses to create larger impacts than from any of these factors alone.

9. *Thresholds will be crossed, leading to large changes in climate and ecosystems.*

There are a variety of thresholds in the climate system and ecosystems. These thresholds determine, for example, the presence of sea ice and permafrost, and the survival of species, from fish to insect pests, with implications for society. With further climate change, the crossing of additional thresholds is expected.

10. *Future climate change and its impacts depend on choices made today.*

The amount and rate of future climate change depend primarily on current and future human-caused emissions of heat-trapping gases and airborne particles. Responses involve reducing emissions to limit future warming, and adapting to the changes that are unavoidable.

TWO

Climate Change Is a Natural Phenomenon

Pat Boone

Pat Boone is a singer, writer, Christian activist, and conservative columnist. In the following perspective Boone asserts that climate change is a natural phenomenon caused by the sun and cites ancient Aztec prophecies and an interview with a solar physicist to support his position. He refers to records showing numerous warm periods in the earth's history that preceded the Industrial Revolution, including the medieval warm period around AD 1100, which Boone says was at least as warm as today. He claims that global warming is a natural phenomenon that recurs at regular intervals. According to Boone, humans prosper during warm periods, so global warming is nothing to be concerned about.

Remember Chicken Little? "The sky is falling! The sky is falling!" Remember?

Well, I'm feeling more strongly all the time that we're experiencing our own re-enactment of that funny little children's story. In that fable, a lot of the barnyard citizens were spooked at first, and the alarm did spread. But by and by, older and wiser creatures spoke up, and by and by, everybody calmed down and resumed their bucolic life.

Some months ago, while driving back home from an engagement, I became fascinated with [talk show host] George Noory's late-night radio interview with a solar physicist, one of a number of very dedicated scientists who actually watch and analyze the sun itself, and its ongoing powerful effects on planet earth.

The Sun Causes Global Warming

This was after former Vice President Al Gore had sounded his alarm in nation after nation about his belief that we're all in serious, imminent danger from global warming. And while the main topic of discussion on Noory's program that night was the remarkable list of prophecies recorded by ancient Aztecs from centuries ago—gleaned somehow from their study and even worship of the sun—the guest scientist brought up the concern solar physicists share about "new, unexplained activity and disturbances" on the surface of that giant fireball in space!

And then he went on to tell his host quite assertively,

This warming in our polar regions, and in other places on this planet, is not unprecedented at all.

It has been recorded in other centuries, and appears to be linked of course to activity on the sun, our source of heat and light. And while it's good to consider how to conserve earth's resources and use them wisely, it's not realistic to think that some rising temperatures in arctic regions and even in our vast seas is attributable to man's use of fossil fuel, and resulting carbon emissions.

Men's actions can and do affect his local environment, but neither man nor machine is powerful enough to seriously disturb our global ecology or our weather patterns. No, the sun itself is the culprit—and we're studying again the ancient Aztec prediction that the year we call 2012 will see cataclysmic changes on our earth, and throughout the solar system.

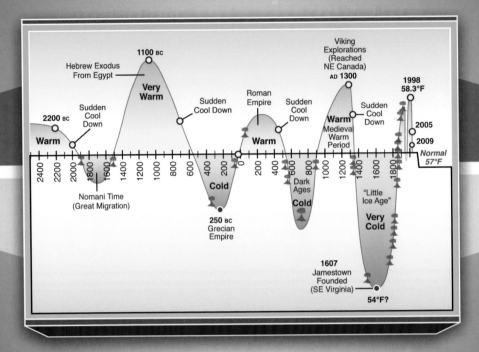

Taken from: http://www.longrangeweather.com/global_temperatures.html.

Global Warming Has Happened Before

I have yet to acquire the book "2012" mentioned that night, but I bring all this up here because of what I've been reading from Dr. S. Fred Singer, representing an organization called CFACT, the Committee For A Constructive Tomorrow. Singer is also a scientist, an atmospheric physicist to be exact, and professor emeritus at the University of Virginia. And Singer begs to differ, and differ deeply, with Al Gore.

Oh, he doesn't deny at all that global warming exists. In fact, he recently co-wrote a book called "*Unstoppable Global Warming: Every 1,500 Years.*" And he, along with a lot of his fellow scientists, substantiate that climate change is a natural phenomenon, that it happens to varying degrees all the time, and that warming cycles just like the one we're experiencing now have happened many times in the past.

He points out that the universal climate warmed steadily between 1900 and 1940, before humanity was using so much energy. But then, climate cooled noticeably from 1940 to 1975, warming again for a short period of time, and since 2000 the best measurements show that the climate has been remaining steady. Yes, for the last three or four years, there have been curious localized melting ice deposits, but the overall average temperature of the earth has changed less than a degree.

The Medieval Warm Period
Was as Warm as Today

There's way too much in Dr. Singer's studies to recount here, but my thanks for such an eye-opening goes to CFACT, a non-profit, strictly non-partisan group, based in Washington, D.C. It was created in 1985 to offer a constructive, fact-based voice on consumer and environmental issues, way before the world began to hear about "global warming." And more wonderful than just having the scientific facts at their disposal, they created in 2001 a student-run organization called Collegians for a Constructive Tomorrow, which is now operating on more than 20 college and university campuses in nine states.

As this organization grows, CFACT collegians from New York to Oregon are sponsoring debates, handing out fact sheets in student centers, and sharing concrete information with fellow students. Through discussions, literature, invited speakers, and events, they're asking the tough questions about the "science" behind Al Gore's much-publicized "warming" scare.

They're causing young people by the thousands, as they prepare to take leadership roles in our future, to consider at least 3000 years of history in which civilizations suffered through cold periods, like the "little ice age" from around 1400 to 1850—when crops failed, people starved and froze, and disease was more deadly. And they learn of the "medieval warm period" around AD 1100, when temperatures were at least as hot as they are now, maybe hotter.

Humans Prosper During Warm Periods

During this time the Vikings discovered Greenland and grew crops there. Life was good in Europe, cathedrals were built, wars and violence decreased, and people generally prospered. And that historical record shows that a warmer period is far better for human beings than a colder one.

Christian activist and political conservative Pat Boone says global warming is good for human beings and that it is a natural phenomenon.

I, for one, am grateful to find out about Dr. Singer, and about CFACT and its collegiate campaign. . . .

Perhaps you'll join me in contributing to the growth of their campaign across our nation. Though many Americans are justifiably concerned about current and future climate conditions, there are those in high positions who want to convince us that human beings are the culprits . . . and that radical elite influence must bring governments to curtail and control our lifestyle.

As always, facts are our friends. We'd do well to gather as many as possible from the most reliable sources. If we substitute fables in their place, we will forever deserve our children's scorn.

THREE

Humans Are Causing Catastrophic Climate Change

James Lovelock

James Lovelock is an independent scientist, author, researcher, and environmentalist who lives in Devon, England. He invented the electron capture detector, which enables detection of atmospheric pollutants at very low levels, and proposed the Gaia hypothesis, which views the earth as a living superorganism regulating itself to maintain favorable conditions for life. Among his published books are *The Revenge of Gaia: Why the Earth Is Fighting Back—and How We Can Still Save Humanity* and *The Vanishing Face of Gaia: A Final Warning*. In the following viewpoint Lovelock looks at the earth (or "Gaia," as he usually refers to it) as a living system and argues that human activity has now seriously unbalanced the earth's natural capacity to maintain conditions favorable for life; as a result, extreme climate change is now inevitable no matter what actions humanity takes. According to the author, over the next century the average global temperature will increase rapidly, so disrupting the earth's ability to support life that the vast majority of humans will die except for a small population surviving at the poles. He suggests that, faced with this catastrophe, the best course of action now is to do whatever can be done to maintain civilization and that there is little time left to act.

Imagine a young policewoman delighted in the fulfilment of her vocation; then imagine her having to tell a family whose child had strayed that he had been found dead, murdered in a nearby wood. Or think of a young physician newly appointed who has to tell you that the biopsy revealed invasion by an aggressive metastasising tumour. Doctors and the police know that many accept the simple awful truth with dignity but others try in vain to deny it.

Whatever the response, the bringers of such bad news rarely become hardened to their task and some dread it. We [in the United Kingdom] have relieved judges of the awesome responsibility of passing the death sentence, but at least they had some comfort from its frequent moral justification. Physicians and the police have no escape from their duty.

This article is the most difficult I have written and for the same reasons. My Gaia theory sees the Earth behaving as if it were alive, and clearly anything alive can enjoy good health, or suffer disease. Gaia has made me a planetary physician and I take my profession seriously, and now I, too, have to bring bad news.

The climate centres around the world, which are the equivalent of the pathology lab of a hospital, have reported the Earth's physical condition, and the climate specialists see it as seriously ill, and soon to pass into a morbid fever that may last as long as 100,000 years. I have to tell you, as members of the Earth's family and an intimate part of it, that you and especially civilisation are in grave danger.

Our planet has kept itself healthy and fit for life, just like an animal does, for most of the more than three billion years of its existence. It was ill luck that we started polluting at a time when the sun is too hot for comfort. We have given Gaia a fever and soon her condition will worsen to a state like a coma. She has been there before and recovered, but it took more than 100,000 years. We are responsible and will suffer the consequences: as the century progresses, the temperature will rise 8 degrees centigrade in temperate regions and 5 degrees in the tropics.

Much of the tropical land mass will become scrub and desert, and will no longer serve for regulation; this adds to the 40 per cent of the Earth's surface we have depleted to feed ourselves.

Curiously, aerosol pollution of the northern hemisphere reduces global warming by reflecting sunlight back to space. This "global dimming" is transient and could disappear in a few days like the smoke that it is, leaving us fully exposed to the heat of the global greenhouse. We are in a fool's climate, accidentally kept cool by smoke, and before this century is over billions of us will die and the few breeding pairs of people that survive will be in the Arctic where the climate remains tolerable.

By failing to see that the Earth regulates its climate and composition, we have blundered into trying to do it ourselves, acting as if we were in charge. By doing this, we condemn ourselves to the worst form of slavery. If we chose to be the stewards of the Earth, then we are responsible for keeping the atmosphere, the ocean and the land surface right for life. A task we would soon find impossible—and something before we treated Gaia so badly, she had freely done for us.

To understand how impossible it is, think about how you would regulate your own temperature or the composition of your blood. Those with failing kidneys know the never-ending daily difficulty of adjusting water, salt and protein intake. The technological fix of dialysis helps but is no replacement for living healthy kidneys.

My new book *The Revenge of Gaia* expands these thoughts, but you still may ask why science took so long to recognise the true nature of the Earth. I think it is because [Charles] Darwin's vision was so good and clear that it has taken until now to digest it. In his time, little was known about the chemistry of the atmosphere and oceans, and there would have been little reason for him to wonder if organisms changed their environment as well as adapting to it.

Had it been known then that life and the environment are closely coupled, Darwin would have seen that evolution involved not just the organisms, but the whole planetary surface. We might then have looked upon the Earth as if it were alive, and known that we cannot pollute the air or use the Earth's skin—its forest and ocean ecosystems—as a mere source of products to feed ourselves and furnish our homes. We would have felt instinctively

© Mike Keefe, The Denver Post & InToon.com

that those ecosystems must be left untouched because they were part of the living Earth.

So what should we do? First, we have to keep in mind the awesome pace of change and realise how little time is left to act; and then each community and nation must find the best use of the resources they have to sustain civilisation for as long as they can. Civilisation is energy-intensive and we cannot turn it off without crashing, so we need the security of a powered descent. On these British Isles, we are used to thinking of all humanity and not just ourselves; environmental change is global, but we have to deal with the consequences here in the UK.

Unfortunately our nation is now so urbanised as to be like a large city and we have only a small acreage of agriculture and forestry. We are dependent on the trading world for sustenance; climate change will deny us regular supplies of food and fuel from overseas.

We could grow enough to feed ourselves on the diet of the Second World War, but the notion that there is land to spare to grow biofuels, or be the site of wind farms, is ludicrous. We will do our best to survive, but sadly I cannot see the United States or the emerging economies of China and India cutting back in time,

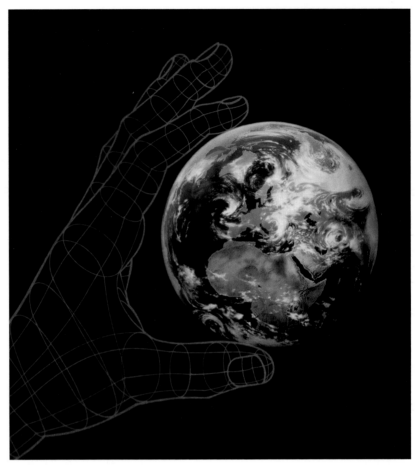

The Gaia hypothesis states that Earth is a living organism that can regulate itself into maintaining favorable conditions for life.

and they are the main source of emissions. The worst will happen and survivors will have to adapt to a hell of a climate.

Perhaps the saddest thing is that Gaia will lose as much or more than we do. Not only will wildlife and whole ecosystems go extinct, but in human civilisation the planet has a precious resource. We are not merely a disease; we are, through our intelligence and communication, the nervous system of the planet. Through us, Gaia has seen herself from space, and begins to know her place in the universe.

We should be the heart and mind of the Earth, not its malady. So let us be brave and cease thinking of human needs and rights alone, and see that we have harmed the living Earth and need to make our peace with Gaia. We must do it while we are still strong enough to negotiate, and not a broken rabble led by brutal war lords. Most of all, we should remember that we are a part of it, and it is indeed our home.

FOUR

Climate Change Skeptics Are Deceiving the Public

Jeffrey Sachs

Jeffrey Sachs is a professor of economics, director of the Earth Institute at Columbia University, and special adviser to United Nations Secretary General Ban Ki-moon. In the following viewpoint Sachs claims that those who deny the scientific consensus on climate change previously attempted to discredit scientific findings on the link between lung cancer and smoking, the depletion of ozone by chlorofluorocarbons, and other threats to human health that since have been proven by science. Sachs refers to two incidents in 2009—one involving stolen e-mails from climate change scientists, the other involving an error in a report issued by the Intergovernmental Panel on Climate Change (IPCC)—and suggests that these are minor factors compared to the overwhelming scientific evidence that climate change is real and presents a dire threat to humanity. According to the author, people with a politically conservative, or right-wing, ideology are attempting to confuse the public on climate change—as they have previously done with other important issues—because to take action on climate change would oppose powerful business interests.

In the weeks before and after the Copenhagen climate change conference last December [2009], the science of climate change came under harsh attack by critics who contend that climate scientists have deliberately suppressed evidence—and that the science itself is severely flawed. The Intergovernmental Panel on Climate Change (IPCC), the global group of experts charged with assessing the state of climate science, has been accused of bias.

The global public is disconcerted by these attacks. If experts cannot agree that there is a climate crisis, why should governments spend billions of dollars to address it?

The fact is that the critics—who are few in number but aggressive in their attacks—are deploying tactics that they have honed

Members of the Intergovernmental Panel on Climate Change (IPCC) meet in May 2010 to review the procedures that produced errors in a report on global warming and that brought into question the panel's credibility.

for more than 25 years. During their long campaign, they have greatly exaggerated scientific disagreements in order to stop action on climate change, with special interests like Exxon Mobil footing the bill.

Many books have recently documented the games played by the climate-change deniers. *Merchants of Doubt*, a new book by Naomi Oreskes and Erik Conway set for release in mid-2010 . . . , will be an authoritative account of their misbehavior. The authors show that the same group of mischief-makers, given a platform by the free-market ideologues of *The Wall Street Journal's* editorial page, has consistently tried to confuse the public and discredit the scientists whose insights are helping to save the world from unintended environmental harm.

Today's campaigners against action on climate change are in many cases backed by the same lobbies, individuals, and organizations that sided with the tobacco industry to discredit the science linking smoking and lung cancer. Later, they fought the scientific evidence that sulfur oxides from coal-fired power plants were causing "acid rain." Then, when it was discovered that certain chemicals called chlorofluorocarbons (CFCs) were causing the depletion of ozone in the atmosphere, the same groups launched a nasty campaign to discredit that science, too.

Later still, the group defended the tobacco giants against charges that second-hand smoke causes cancer and other diseases. And then, starting mainly in the 1980s, this same group took on the battle against climate change.

What is amazing is that, although these attacks on science have been wrong for 30 years, they still sow doubts about established facts. The truth is that there is big money backing the climate-change deniers, whether it is companies that don't want to pay the extra costs of regulation, or free-market ideologues opposed to any government controls.

The latest round of attacks involves two episodes. The first was the hacking of a climate-change research center in England. The emails that were stolen suggested a lack of forthrightness in the presentation of some climate data. Whatever the details of this

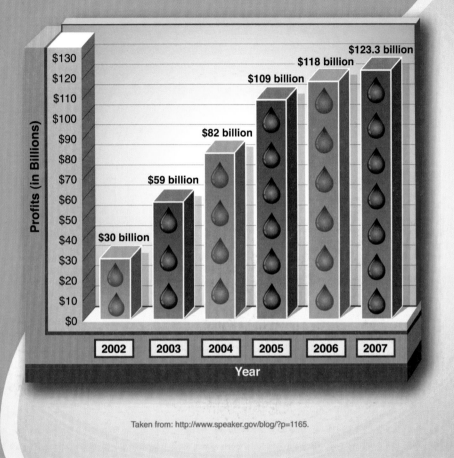

specific case, the studies in question represent a tiny fraction of the overwhelming scientific evidence that points to the reality and urgency of man-made climate change.

The second issue was a blatant error concerning glaciers that appeared in a major IPCC report. Here it should be understood that the IPCC issues thousands of pages of text. There are, no doubt, errors in those pages. But errors in the midst of a vast and complex report by the IPCC point to the inevitability of human shortcomings, not to any fundamental flaws in climate science.

When the emails and the IPCC error were brought to light, editorial writers at *The Wall Street Journal* launched a vicious campaign describing climate science as a hoax and a conspiracy. They claimed that scientists were fabricating evidence in order to obtain government research grants—a ludicrous accusation, I thought at the time, given that the scientists under attack have devoted their lives to finding the truth, and have certainly not become rich relative to their peers in finance and business.

But then I recalled that this line of attack—charging a scientific conspiracy to drum up "business" for science—was almost identical to that used by *The Wall Street Journal* and others in the past, when they fought controls on tobacco, acid rain, ozone depletion, second-hand smoke, and other dangerous pollutants. In other words, their arguments were systematic and contrived, not at all original to the circumstances.

We are witnessing a predictable process by ideologues and right-wing think tanks and publications to discredit the scientific process. Their arguments have been repeatedly disproved for 30 years—time after time—but their aggressive methods of public propaganda succeed in causing delay and confusion.

Climate change science is a wondrous intellectual activity. Great scientific minds have learned over the course of many decades to "read" the Earth's history, in order to understand how the climate system works. They have deployed brilliant physics, biology, and instrumentation (such as satellites reading detailed features of the Earth's systems) in order to advance our understanding.

And the message is clear: large-scale use of oil, coal, and gas is threatening the biology and chemistry of the planet. We are fueling dangerous changes in Earth's climate and ocean chemistry, giving rise to extreme storms, droughts, and other hazards that will damage the food supply and the quality of life of the planet.

The IPCC and the climate scientists are telling us a crucial message. We need urgently to transform our energy, transport, food, industrial, and construction systems to reduce the dangerous human impact on the climate. It is our responsibility to listen, to understand the message, and then to act.

FIVE

Climate Change Scientists Are to Blame for Increasing Public Doubt

Anne McElvoy

Anne McElvoy is executive editor of the *Evening Standard*, a London newspaper, and writes a weekly political column for that paper. In the following viewpoint McElvoy discusses a scandal in which e-mails from climate scientists were released to the public by hackers. According to the author, the e-mails implied that the scientists were using tricks and misleading information to make their case that climate change is a serious problem. She compares the conduct of these scientists with that of politicians who she says exaggerated and distorted the evidence of Iraq's possession of weapons of mass destruction in order to justify invading that country. McElvoy suggests that while there is abundant evidence that climate change must be taken seriously, the scientists undermine their case when they use misleading language and avoid public scrutiny.

Rule of modern life: never annoy a climate change apostle. They don't take kindly to it and get ratty, because they are not used to it. Now and again, if you hold a strong belief, it is quite normal for something to come along that shakes the foundations of what you think.

It is part of life and very much part of science. Indeed, the entire rational scientific method is based on a readiness to review and correct errors, large or small, and to accept challenges to what is already known.

It is what makes it so valuable. In the global warming debate, it is all we have to rely on. The rest is, you might say, just hot air. That is why the likes of Professor Phil Jones, director of the University of East Anglia's Climatic Research Unit, boasting in leaked emails of using "Mike's Nature trick . . . to hide the decline" (in recent recorded temperatures), were playing such a foolish game.

That, plus an aversion to openness and the dismissive reaction to scepticism about their claims, must be taken, seriously.

Climate Scientists Are Setting a Bad Example

Yet the response has been an evasive flippancy, with renowned ecowriters parodying the affair, or merely saying both sides in the global warming argument are prone to distortion and exaggeration.

But hang on: these are people who use the scientific method to make the case that climate change is so important that countries (and individuals) should be prepared to make major sacrifices to move to a low-carbon economy. They want their work to lead to change. That brings with it a special duty not to resort to shortcuts—however trivial.

Professor Jones was not using the language of sober science but the self-congratulation of the believer who thinks a fast one can be pulled or a corner cut in order to further his own case.

Professor Bob Watson, a Defra [Department for Environment, Food and Rural Affairs in Britain] adviser on the issue and fellow UEA [University of East Anglia] scientist, explained (sort of) on

Americans Less Sure About Scientists' Belief in Global Warming

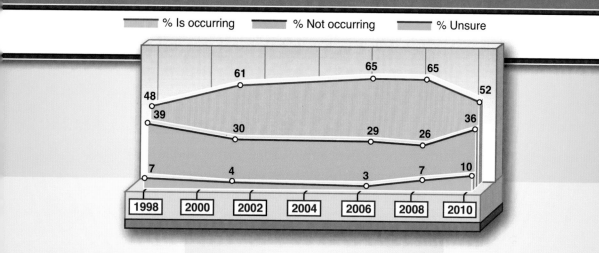

Which one of the following statements do you think is most accurate—most scientists believe that global warming is occurring, most scientists believe that global warming is not occurring, or most scientists are unsure about whether global warming is occurring or not?

% Is occurring   % Not occurring   % Unsure

Taken from: "Americans' Global Warming Concerns Continue to Drop," Gallup.com, March 11, 2010.

Newsnight: "They used the word 'trick' as an expression of mathematical approach . . . clearly they need to think through how to express the English language much clearer." I'll say. It doesn't address the broader point, though, which is about mentality and impression of a general group-think.

Some of the mails have the tone and assumption of people who do not relish challenge and treat critical scrutiny as something annoying.

They were apparently in favour of deleting departmental emails rather than succumb to the glare of others probing into the department under the Freedom of Information Act.

The institute is invariably referred to as "respected" in newspapers, though at this rate, it won't be for much longer.

Science Should Be Open to Public Scrutiny

Professor Watson's prime concern is "how the computer was hacked into". How awfully like listening to stodgy Whitehall [British government] officials taking umbrage at requests to see controversial memos, or MPs [members of Parliament] complaining about the discs of their expenses being sold. Public interest lies in knowing what is being quietly said on the inside—not in punishing those who brought it to light.

For a layman to come to a view on the exact degree of global warming, its causes and what needs to be done to remedy it is notoriously difficult.

We can apply common sense but we ultimately fall back on a faith in the evidence that others gather and assess for us. That entails a relationship of trust between scientists and the public that should not be so lightly squandered.

While I was sitting in the Iraq inquiry this week [late November 2004], the example of the [British prime minister Tony] Blair government's treatment of the WMD [weapons of mass destruction] evidence in 2003 came to mind. Nothing I have seen since convinces me that the Government did not have reasonable grounds for thinking [former Iraqi president] Saddam [Hussein] still had WMD.

But the evidence base was nowhere near wide enough for the weight put on it for political reasons. When that emerged, Mr Blair's credibility on the matter was smashed for good.

That is a warning from history. I squirmed when reading a researcher describe as a "travesty" that he can't prove the temperature rise he wants to confirm: the fact that he wants a certain result should make him more cautious.

The Public Distrusts Experts

Those who want radical action at the Copenhagen summit on climate change [in Denmark in December 2009] can argue with justification that they are trying to do us all a favour by highlighting the clear and present danger of global warming and demanding measures to address it.

If you subtract those Greens who are basically a reincarnation of Left-wing anti-capitalists and those who are hostile to the very idea of economic growth, you're left with a considerable body of informed evidence that says climate change should be a priority for this generation.

Some scientists aligned to this view are absolutely scrupulous in their methods, and others are plainly campaigners first and scientists second (and indeed probably chose to be researchers in this field on grounds of conviction). The UEA case risks blurring that vital line.

Professor Bob Watson explains to an inquiry that the use of the word "trick" in the IPCC's e-mails was an expression of a mathmatical approach and not a deliberate attempt to deceive the public about global warming.

The public has learned to distrust experts—in an era when we know more than our trusting forebears, we've seen forensic scientists and doctors squirm under the revelation that their treasured evidence was flawed and the results misleading. "Don't you think it's scary," a minister said to me yesterday, "that 55 per cent of people don't believe global warming is man-made?" Well, no, I don't. It is the job of those who know more about it to convince us with rigour and argument that their assessment is correct and should be the basis of what we do—and stop doing.

The whole rhetoric of calling the unconvinced "deniers", the resort to the language of a "trick" and "travesty" is part of a sloppy intellectual culture which will, in the end, undermine the very achievements of genuine climate science and its influence.

Because I am not a member of the Doubter's Church of Lord Lawson [a British conservative politician well known for his skeptical stance on climate change], the refusal to treat global warming as a major issue seems to me an unwise risk to take with all our futures.

But if the scientists and their uncritical supporters can't see that they have only themselves to blame for increasing doubt and distrust, perhaps they're not so clever after all.

SIX

A Drastic Reduction of Greenhouse Gas Emissions Is Needed to Prevent Climate Change

Ronnie Cummins and Will Allen

Ronnie Cummins is an organizer, writer, activist, and the international director of the Organic Consumers Association (OCA). Will Allen is a community organizer, activist, writer and policy advisor for the OCA. In the following viewpoint, the authors argue that major cuts in greenhouse gas emissions must happen immediately to avoid catastrophic climate change. The only way this is going to happen, they contend, is if the United States leads by example by redirecting huge amounts of money to reorganize society in a more sustainable way. They say that a grassroots movement that will assist on the changes needed for human survival is gaining momentum. American consumers are largely responsible for global warming, according to Allen and Cummins, therefore Americans will have to change their way of life in order to bring emissions of greenhouse gases to a sustainable level. While the amount of money needed for these changes is large—the authors claim that it is equivalent to the Pentagon budget—it is minor in comparison to recent bailouts for Wall Street investment companies and other corporations.

The climate, energy, and political catastrophe we are facing is mind-boggling and frightening. Yet there is still time to save ourselves, to move beyond psychological denial, despair, or false optimism. There is still hope if we are willing to confront the hydra-headed monsters that block our path, and move ahead with a decisive plan of action. The inspirational message we need to deliver is that we're not just talking about drastically reducing fossil fuel use and greenhouse gas (GHG) pollution, but rebuilding society, creating in effect a New Woman and a New Man for the 21st Century. What we are witnessing are the early stages of a mass grassroots consciousness-raising and taking back of power from out-of-control corporations, banks, corporate-controlled media, and politicians. This cultural and political revolution will empower us to to carry out a deep and profound retrofitting of industry, government, education, health care, housing, neighborhoods, transportation, food and farming systems, as well as our diets and lifestyles.

A Cultural and Political Revolution

The scale of human and physical resources needed to turn our current suicide economy into a green economy is daunting, but absolutely necessary and achievable. The only viable roadmap for survival—an 80–90% reduction in fossil fuel use and greenhouse gas (GHG) emissions by 2050—means we must force a drastic reduction in military spending (current wars and military spending are costing us almost one trillion dollars a year). We must tax the rich and the greenhouse gas polluters, and bring our out-of-control politicians, banks, Federal Reserve System, and corporations to heel.

The good news . . . , is that this 21st Century green economy will not only stabilize the climate, but enable us to retrain and reemploy the U.S. workforce, including low-income youth and 16–25 million unemployed workers, as building retrofitters, solar and wind installers, recyclers, organic gardeners, farmers, nutritionists, holistic health care providers, and other green economy workers.

The negotiators and heads of state at the December 2009 Copenhagen Climate negotiations abandoned the summit with literally no agreement on meaningful greenhouse gas (carbon dioxide, nitrous oxide, methane) reduction, and little or no acknowledgement of the major role that industrial (non-organic) food and farming practices play in global warming. Unfortunately the statements and behavior of Copenhagen delegates, and the enormous divisions between the Global South [the developing nations that are mostly in the Southern Hemisphere] and the industrialized nations, make it clear that galvanizing a legally binding international agreement to drastically reduce greenhouse gas pollution will be a protracted and difficult struggle.

Major Cuts in Emissions Need to Start Now

China and the United States are equally and jointly responsible for more than 40% of the current global climate destabilizing GHGs. China's emissions arise from 20% of the world's population. U.S. emissions come from 5%. Although China, India, Mexico, Brazil and other developing nations are responsible for a growing discharge of GHGs, most of the greenhouse gasses in the atmosphere and oceans today are directly attributable to the United States and Europe's industrial and transportation emissions since the early 1900s.

From an ethical, legal, and survival perspective, North America, E.U. [the European Union] and Japan must lead the way. To avoid a disastrous rise in global temperature (a literal climate holocaust), the wealthy, highly industrialized nations must acknowledge the seriousness of the crisis, cut their emissions, and stop playing blame and denial games with China, India, Brazil, Mexico, South Africa and other developing nations. Major cuts by the developed nations need to start now, and they need to be deep, not 7% as President [Barack] Obama proposed in Copenhagen, nor the 20% that the E.U. offered.

The hour is late. Leading climate scientists such as James Hansen are literally shouting at the top of their lungs that the world needs to reduce emissions by 20–40% as soon as possible,

Many leading climate scientists, such as James Hansen, director of NASA's Goddard Institute, say the world must reduce carbon emissions by 20–40 percent as soon as possible and by 80–90 percent by 2050 to avoid a global disaster.

and 80–90% by the year 2050, if we are to avoid climate chaos, crop failures, endless wars, melting of the polar icecaps, and a disastrous rise in ocean levels. Either we radically reduce CO_2 [carbon dioxide] and carbon dioxide equivalent (CO_2e, which includes all GHGs, not just CO_2) pollutants (currently at 390 parts per million [ppm] and rising 2 ppm per year) to 350 ppm, including agriculture-derived methane and nitrous oxide pollution, or else survival for the present and future generations is in jeopardy. As scientists warned at Copenhagen, business as usual and a corresponding 7–8.6 degree Fahrenheit rise in global temperatures means that the carrying capacity of the Earth in 2100 will be reduced to one billion people. Under this hellish scenario, billions will die of thirst, cold, heat, disease, war, and starvation.

The United States Must Lead by Example

If the U.S. significantly reduces greenhouse gas emissions, other countries will follow. One hopeful sign is the recent EPA [Environmental Protection Agency] announcement that it intends to regulate greenhouse gases as pollutants under the Clean Air Act. Unfortunately we are going to have to put tremendous pressure on elected public officials to force the EPA to crack down on GHG polluters (including industrial farms and food processors). Public pressure is especially critical since "just say no" Congressmen—both Democrats and Republicans—along with agribusiness, real estate developers, the construction industry, and the fossil fuel lobby appear determined to maintain "business as usual."

During the [President George W.] Bush years, scientific warnings and public demonstrations against global warming were ignored or trivialized, even though many of our protests were large and well organized. Now, in theory, we finally have a Congressional majority and a President [Obama] who claim to be willing to listen and take action to stop global warming. But in order to get their attention, and move from small change to major change, we are going to have to turn up the volume. We have to stop thinking that things are going to get better because Obama is right-minded. Things are going to get better if and when we force Obama and our out-of-control politicians and corporations to bend to the people's will.

Instead of the weak "cap and trade" bill supported by Wall Street speculators, and passed by the House, we need a real tax on GHG pollution. Yes, we can and must directly rebate working class and poor people for increased energy costs, but hundreds of billions of dollars in GHG and corporate taxes annually must be earmarked over the next decade for green infrastructure development, including a new electric grid, a mass transition to organic agriculture, mass transit upgrades, deep retrofitting of the nation's five million commercial and 83 million residential buildings, and a crash program of alternative energy research and development.

We must continue to expose the worst greenhouse gas polluters, such as utilities companies, petrochemical corporations, car manufacturers, coal and mining companies, the construction industry, and corporate agribusiness, and demand that they begin to retool their industries immediately. We must move beyond polite protest and scattered dissent and dramatically take our message to the streets and the corporate suites, Congress, state legislatures, and our local governments.

Consumers Responsible for Emissions

We all know in general that cars, trucks, coal and power plants, household heating and cooling, and manufacturing industries spew a majority of the greenhouse gasses into the atmosphere and the oceans. But did you know that U.S. household use of fossil fuels (housing, transportation, and food) accounts for 67% of total energy consumption and 67% of GHG's emitted?

Heating, lighting, and cooling our poorly insulated and designed 113 million homes and apartments and running our electrical and gas appliances consumes 26.6% of total U.S. fossil fuels.

Cruising in our gas guzzling (averaging 22 miles per gallon) and underutilized cars (average 1.4 passengers per journey) burns up another 23.4% of energy.

Eating highly processed and packaged foods and animal products, produced on chemical and energy-intensive factory-style

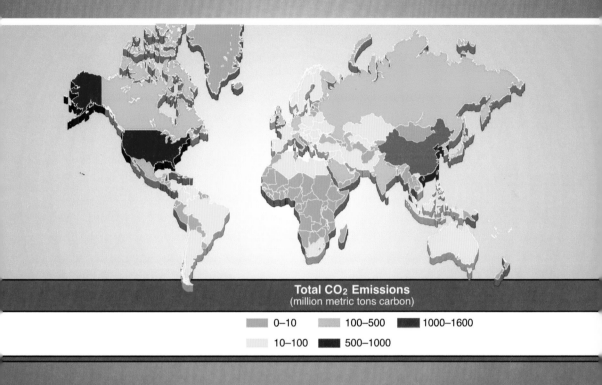

Total CO₂ Greenhouse Gas Emissions by Country, 2000

Total CO2 Emissions
(million metric tons carbon)

0–10	100–500	1000–1600
10–100	500–1000	

Taken from: http://www.clemson.edu.

farms, transported over long distances, and throwing our waste foods into the garbage (rather than composting them) eats up another 17.3% of the nation's energy.

The average U.S. citizen generates 19.6 tons of climate destabilizing greenhouse gases every year, more than twice as much as the European Union and Japan (9.3 tons per capita), and 7.3 times as much as the developing world (2.7 tons per capita).

Saving the United States from Climate Chaos

The estimated costs over the next 40–50 years to replace coal and natural gas with solar and wind in electricity generation, at current levels of use, is $15 trillion (which is about the equivalent of U.S. GNP [gross national product] for one year).

We must reduce fossil fuel use by 80–90% in the nation's five million commercial and 83 million residential buildings (which currently use up 40% . . . of our total energy), including reducing building size, changing lighting and windows, making wall, ceilings and floors as thick and as airtight as possible . . . , and placing furnaces and ductwork inside the retrofitted space. The estimated costs for this in future decades will amount to another $10–15 trillion. . . .

Converting from our current energy and chemical/GMO [genetically modified organism]–intensive food and farming system (which currently accounts for 35% of our greenhouse gases and $800 billion in diet-related health care costs annually) to one which is organic, relocalized, energy-efficient, and carbon sequestering, will cost at least another $100 billion per year, or $5 trillion over 50 years.

Rebuilding our mass transit systems and reorganizing personal transportation (5–15 people in high-mileage "smart jitneys" and electric cars and vans instead of 1.4 passengers in gas guzzlers, along with a massive increase in bicycle use) will cost us at least another $100 billion a year, or $5 trillion over 50 years.

Necessary Changes Are Affordable

In other words we need to start redirecting $700 billion a year in federal expenditures away from war and corporate welfare, offer training and jobs in a giant green jobs program (similar to the Works Project Administration program of the New Deal era in the 1930s), and build a new green, full-employment economy. Where are we going to get this money? Not by raising taxes on working people and the poor, but by taxing the rich and the greenhouse gas polluting corporations, and guaranteeing loans from a new citizen-controlled Federal Reserve and banking system. . . .

Can we afford $700 billion per year? Obviously we can, although shortsighted, unsustainable corporate profits will no doubt suffer.

Keep in mind that the Pentagon budget, not including the wars for oil and strategic resources in Afghanistan and Iraq, will cost us over $700 billion dollars this year [2010]. And don't forget that Obama and his advisors recently handed over approximately $12 trillion in subsidies and grants to the Wall Street criminals and pathological kleptomaniacs who rule our out-of-control financial system. Clearly, what we are proposing is chump-change compared to our recent corporate giveaways.

Honest businesses, homeowners, consumers, farmers and industries that reduce their carbon footprint and help develop the green economy can and should receive substantial tax credits. Speculators, mercenaries, toxic polluters, and Masters of War can go to financial hell, where they belong.

SEVEN

An Emissions Reduction Strategy Would Cause More Harm than Climate Change Would

Oliver Kamm

Oliver Kamm is a British writer and an opinion columnist for the *Times*, a London newspaper. He was previously an investment banker and cofounder of an asset management firm. In the following viewpoint, Kamm argues that it is misguided to oppose economic growth in the name of saving the environment. He feels that environmentalism lacks a sense of priorities, failing to address nonenvironmental causes of suffering such as poverty in the developing world. According to the author, people value the environment more when their basic needs are met. Encouraging economic growth in developing nations, rather than stifling it, will eventually lead to a healthier, more sustainable environment, he contends.

I took part in a Radio 3 [a British radio station] discussion recently about the new age of austerity. A poet on the programme argued for the simple virtues. The recession, he said, would give consumers in rich societies an opportunity to rediscover thrift and conservation. The future of the planet depended on a curb to materialism and acquisitiveness.

That message is today's green orthodoxy, and its advocates have a reassuring air of humanitarian concern. But it is a reactionary notion. To the student of economic history, it recalls nothing so much as the pocket sermons of the original do-nothing Republican, President Herbert Hoover. As the global economy succumbed to the Great Depression, Hoover looked on the bright side of financial panic. "It will purge the rottenness out of the system," he declared. "High costs of living and high living will come down. People will work harder, live a more moral life."

Anti-materialism has perennial appeal. . . . "This time around," writes a founder of [the environmental organization] Greenpeace International, "we're not going to recover from global recession by consuming more resources and energy. Growth cannot solve the problems created by growth.". . .

A recession is, by definition, consecutive quarters of negative growth. Personal consumption is the biggest component of national income. If we consume more, then recovery will come. The question that less strident environmentalists raise is whether the use of resources can be made sustainable, so that present and future human needs are met while the environment is preserved. That sounds a moderate aim but it's full of problems.

Environmentalism Lacks a Sense of Priorities

Green campaigners are rightly concerned with environmental degradation. There is copious evidence of global warming due to man-made emissions of carbon dioxide and other gases that trap heat. The pace of glacial retreat and a rise in sea levels confirm it. The journalists and politicians who take issue with the science are no more credible than the ones (sometimes the same people) who dispute [the evolutionary theory of Charles] Darwin. Climate change poses not only environmental hazards. The desperately poor state of Bangladesh faces twin threats of catastrophic flooding and Islamist militancy. Amid the devastation of low-lying areas and a mass flight to higher ground, malevolent extremism might thrive.

For all that, environmentalism is a flawed idea. Its weakness is not that it lacks justice, but that it lacks a sense of priorities. How do you rank global warming relative to women's rights in Afghanistan or the prevention of genocide in Darfur? "Save the planet" is an exhortation, not a policy, and it doesn't get you far. In particular, it gives no guidance on how to weigh present needs, such as eradicating poverty in the developing world, against future constraints on natural resources. In short, it does not deal with trade-offs. That is a big omission.

If the planet faced catastrophe on the scale envisaged by the theorists of the "limits to growth", then all public policy ought indeed to be subordinated to preventing it. But not even greens, beyond a few dystopian survivalists, argue that case. They instead invoke the Precautionary Principle (the capital letters are important, apparently.)

An Overly Cautious Approach Stifles Innovation

Oddly, this has no fixed definition but is cited widely and vaguely by organisations such as Unesco [United Nations Educational, Scientific, and Cultural Organization] as a strategy for guarding against serious, and especially irreversible, damage to natural resources. The problem, as Dick Taverne, the Liberal Democrat peer [a British politician], has pointed out, is that because the Precautionary Principle "operates asymmetrically and emphasises possible harm, not benefit, it is bound to tilt the balance against innovation". And if there is one resource that is almost infinitely renewable, it is human inventiveness.

It is not fanciful to expect substitutes for fossil fuels to be developed, to the benefit of the environment. It has happened continually. The alternative to environmentalist prescriptions is not the Pollyanna Principle [viewing things in too positive a light]. It is a recognition that our knowledge of the effects of climate change is limited, and that solutions do occur as innovation substitutes new products for old. If we elevate environmental concerns above all other goals, as a matter of policy, then there will be costs. Greens should be open that the biggest costs will almost inevitably be borne by the poorest people.

Fundamental Challenges of Survival and Development

- **2.5 billion** people still lack access to improved sanitation facilities.

- **1 billion** children are deprived of one or more services essential to survival and development

- **148 million** under-fives in developing regions are underweight for their age.

- **101 million** children are not attending primary school, with more girls than boys missing out.

- **22 million** infants are not protected from diseases by routine immunization.

- **8.8 million** children worldwide died before their fifth birthday in 2008.

Taken from: UNICEF, "State of the World's Children," November 2009.

As the international economy recovers, policymakers will seek to stimulate domestic demand in the rapidly industrialising nations of China and India. Making people richer in previously poor nations is a good thing. But it will increase pollution and carbon emissions.

The relationship between living standards and pollution is complex. Some economists believe the relationship is like an inverted U-curve, in which pollution increases as per capita incomes in a developing country increase, but then declines once a certain standard of living is reached.

It makes intuitive sense that people value the environment more when they have enough to eat and various material wants are satisfied.

Economic Growth Will Lead to a Cleaner Environment

If this is right, then the most effective long-term route to preserving the environment will be to encourage growth in the developing world. Insisting on unrealistic pollution targets now will work against that goal. But in any event, there is a short-run trade-off between environmental standards and an increase in economic welfare in the developing world.

Critics of the environmentalists' position on climate change point out that "saving the planet" is only an exhortation and not an actual policy that addresses economic problems.

It is far from obvious that the environment takes precedence. And there are ominous protectionist currents in green campaigns. The former Vice-President Al Gore has argued that "weak and ineffectual enforcement of pollution control measures should also be included in the definition of unfair trading practices".

No, they shouldn't. Integration into the global trading system benefits poor countries. They can specialise in what they produce, become more productive and thereby get richer.

That is also the long-term route to a cleaner environment. Closed economies in the developing world do not benefit from the advanced clean technologies used by multinational companies. China under Mao [Tse-tung] was an extreme case of a self-sufficient economy that emphasised local production and it was an environmental disaster. A blast furnace in every village produced unusable steel and toxic fumes. Growth and open trade are the route to a better quality of life. It is a surpassing irony that today's green evangelists won't recognise it.

When they have enough to eat, people value the environment more.

EIGHT

Geoengineering Is the Solution to Climate Change

Alan AtKisson

Alan AtKisson is a speaker, musician, and environmental consultant who has written two books on sustainability: *Believing Cassandra: An Optimist Looks at a Pessimist's World* and *The ISIS Agreement: How Sustainability Can Improve Organizational Performance and Transform the World*. In the following viewpoint AtKisson claims that climate change has already become so serious that humans must start engineering the climate, or geoengineering, to prevent catastrophic effects of global warming. The author refers to a recently discovered phenomenon called "global dimming," a process whereby industrial pollution has been blocking out a significant percentage of solar radiation, thus masking much of the global warming that has already occurred. AtKisson claims that through global dimming society has already started large-scale geoengineering, but in an unconscious way. He suggests that humanity start taking conscious control of the climate through deliberate geoengineering projects, to counteract the effects of the harm already caused to the earth's natural balance.

[B]ritish environmentalist] James Lovelock's doomsday message ("The Earth is about to catch a morbid fever that may last as long as 100,000 years," *The Independent*, 16 February 2006, page 1) is, one fervently hopes, a prediction whose purpose is not to dispel hope, but to act as a last desperate plea for action, at the scale that is required to save the balance of natural systems on Earth. His book, *The Revenge of Gaia* (2006), had yet to come out, but from the newspaper articles summarizing his argument, one notes that his prediction is based on assumptions that include (1) that the US and China will not control their carbon emissions in time, and (2) that we will not take otherwise sufficient action, globally, to avert the worst-case scenario of 5-to-8 degree Celsius global warming. If Lovelock can be proven wrong on both counts, one would conclude, then nature and civilization are both saved.

The only way to prove Lovelock wrong is to take him seriously, and prove him wrong—by acting to change the world, so that these assumptions and conclusions no longer hold.

Global Warming Could Suddenly Accelerate

About the urgency and credibility of Lovelock's alarming pronouncement, I personally have no doubt. A year ago [in 2005], when the news about global dimming—which has been dampening the effect of global warming, by shading out 10–30% of the sun's rays with our industrial smoke—was reported in the scientific press, I was in Australia on a speaking tour. This news, I remember saying to government officials and others there, makes the situation far graver than we previously understood it to be. If the smoke disappears, as it mostly did over the skies of the United States after 9/11, the earth immediately heats up even more (as data collected during those days showed rather conclusively). It is possible, verging on likely, that Europe's heat waves were exacerbated by the fact that Europe has better air quality controls, thus reducing the shading effect of particulates. "Global dimming" is partly saving us from global warming.

British environmentalist James Lovelock, creator of the Gaia hypothesis, with the electron capture detector he built to measure chlorofluorocabons (CFCs) in the atmosphere.

Even with that dimming effect, the level of warming is already dangerous. And there are other feedback mechanisms—such as the release of methane from melting tundra—that are also lurking in the all-too-likely future, ready to accelerate warming still further. We are stuck in a dilemma, I noted to clients and audiences, far stickier than even the most concerned among us realize. We cannot afford to "clean the skies" too much right now, until we have come up with some other way to dampen the warming effect, or to change the carbon balance in the atmosphere. This is a terribly ironic, but inevitable and logical, conclusion.

Climate "Mega-Engineering" Projects Are Controversial

Of course, I was just a consultant and author, and no scientist. So I confined my great worries to small lecture halls and to dialogue with professional colleagues and friends in the scientific and policy communities. Now Lovelock—whose reputation as a scientist has grown enormously over the years, giving him a status approaching that of [evolutionary biologist Charles] Darwin—has made the world a bit safer for these public reflections. And he has also elevated the urgency of a great ethical debate.

In environment, conservation, and sustainability circles, it is traditional to view our ethical responsibility to nature in terms of leaving it alone, or actively preserving it as it is, unchanged. This ethic is applied to both small systems, like a patch of forest, and large ones, such as the global climate. Debates about "mega-engineering" the climate, which might include things like fertilizing the oceans (so that plankton will absorb more CO_2) and various carbon sequestration technologies, are enormously heated. We must not tamper with natural systems at that scale, goes the anti-engineering argument, because we do not understand these systems well enough. We could set forces in motion that destroy all or part of an ecosystem, or even threaten to undermine an important food source for humans.

I respect that argument a great deal, and I sympathize with the spirit of it. Unfortunately, it is no longer tenable as a strategy, and this makes it untenable ethically as well.

When it comes to the atmosphere and its role in regulating global temperatures, we have already set forces in motion on a scale so great that we still, even after all these years of scientific study and international debate, do not comprehend how great a change we have already created. A "hands-off" ethic is entirely appropriate when keeping our hands off nature is what will save it. But it is too late for that. Keeping our hands off the system, as conditions are now, spells doom. The only way for us to save vast tracts of nature now—and according to Lovelock, civilization itself—is to put our hands to work at managing the climate system, as intensively as we can.

Let's start with global dimming. We must accept that we now have an ethical responsibility to manage this effect on a global scale. It is not a natural effect; indeed, it is entirely accidental and human-caused, the equivalent of a continuous large volcanic eruption. (Mount Pinatubo's expulsion of dust into the atmosphere similarly shaded the planet from global warming in the 1990s.) And yet global dimming is part of our current, entirely unconscious, "climate management strategy." We must consider whether we actually need *more* of it, to counter the warming effects we are already fated to experience because of the great delays in the climate system. (Even if we stopped emitting CO_2 today, temperatures would continue to rise for many years to come.)

I am not proposing that we stoke up our coal-fired power plants and increase the number of planes flying just to shade the planet. I am, however, proposing that we must take seriously our responsibility to monitor and actively manage this effect, at a global level, and even to investigate whether there are other ways to shade the planet without contributing to even more global warming through increased CO_2 and other emissions, without increasing acid rain from smoke deposition, and the like.

The Point of No Return Has Been Passed

In sum, we must become conscious of the fact that *we are already mega-engineering the planet*, on an absolutely enormous scale—and doing it quite unconsciously and very, very badly. The nature of our debates must now switch from "Should we tamper with these things?" to "How best do we tamper with them, in order to preserve both nature and the needs of human life?"

Mega-engineering the planet does not release us from the obligation to push harder on changes in our high-consumption lifestyles, perverse economic incentives, insufficient sustainable development in poor areas and the like. Indeed, our responsibility to attend earnestly to such things is only increased with every passing day. We need to engage every possible and humane lever of change available to us ranging from individual conviction that change is necessary, to global treaties to secure purposeful collaboration among nations. The United States and China, as the world's largest emitters of greenhouse gasses, have a special responsibility in this regard.

But in our thinking and action on climate change, we can no longer avoid the fact that we are past a point of no return. Pandora's box is not just open, but long since emptied. Genuine hope is to be found not in doing less tampering with the climate, but in doing far more: far more regulation of carbon dioxide emissions, with market and non-market mechanisms. Far more research into carbon sequestration. Far more development

Global Dimming Is Concealing the Extent of Global Warming

Industrial pollution has been shielding the earth from 10–30 percent of the sun's rays. This "global dimming" effect has mitigated the full scale of global warming that has already occurred.

Taken from: Alan AtKisson, "We Must Mega-Engineer," January 19, 2005.

of alternative energy prospects. Far more willingness to imagine strategies that currently sound like science fiction—such as building space-based solar energy arrays that would simultaneously power the planet, and partially shade us from the sun, so that we can regulate global temperatures long enough to learn how to restore a more "natural," self-regulating, life-sustaining balance to the global atmosphere.

Lovelock revolutionized the life sciences by demonstrating that the entire Earth is a living mechanism, working in systemic harmony to maintain the conditions for life itself. We are a product of that system. Currently, we are, as he puts it, Gaia's malady [illness], and we have disrupted its regulating mechanisms far beyond their capacity to self-repair in time to save the things we love.

So we must repair them. We have it in our power to become the regulating consciousness of this great living spherical fabric of life. We have the power to regulate the climate: that power is evident in the destruction we have already caused, unconsciously. We must now, with all due haste and urgency, begin to take our new role as planetary managers and engineers far more seriously, so that we learn to do it well.

James Lovelock, whose Gaia Hypothesis was at first dismissed, was ultimately proven right, because he accurately described something that was demonstrably true, but which science had previously failed to see. But the future is not yet a fact. We must now do everything in our power to prove this great scientist wrong—not by dismissing his warning, but by heeding it.

NINE

Geoengineering Could Be Disastrous

Alex Steffen

Alex Steffen is a writer, public speaker, and futurist and is the editor and cofounder of the online magazine Worldchanging since its inception in 2003, as well as editor of the book *Worldchanging: A User's Guide for the 21st Century.* In the following viewpoint, Steffen argues that schemes to engineer the climate of the earth—geoengineering—are profoundly dangerous. In his opinion, the term geo-engineering could be more accurately called geo-experimentation or geo-gambling because not enough is known about the impacts on the climate systems meant to be changed to precisely affect them; Steffen also believes that unintended harmful consequences are a likely result of the geoengineering ideas that have been proposed. For example, the idea of causing the oceans to absorb more carbon dioxide would make the oceans more acidic, which is another serious threat to life on earth. According to the author, this is an example of "carbon blindness," focusing so narrowly on the problem of carbon dioxide that other environmental threats are ignored completely. The author concludes that humankind has other means to address climate change, and geoengineering is far too risky to be seriously considered.

Alex Steffen, "Why Geo-Engineering Is a Debate Whose Time Has Gone," Worldchanging.com, December 21, 2007. © 2007 Worldchanging. Reproduced by permission.

With some regularity these days, I get calls from reporters wanting to know my thoughts about various schemes for attempting to use enormous technofixes—vast space mirrors, mountains of iron filings dumped into the oceans, newly planted forests of trees gene-hacked to suck in more carbon dioxide, intentionally filling the atmosphere with sulfate pollution (creating a sort of artificial volcano), etc.—to combat climate change. And, increasingly, my opinion has grown stronger: they're all dumb, dangerous ideas.

Large mirrors designed to shield Earth from the sun in an attempt to control climate change are examples of geoengineering.

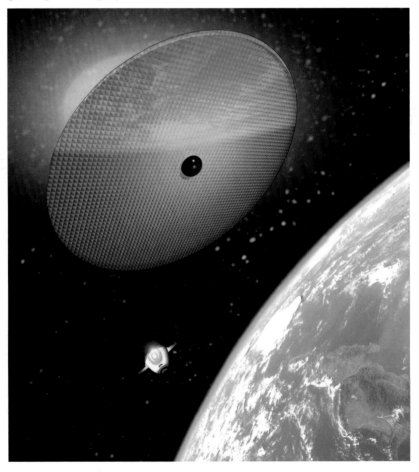

I generally believe we ought to keep an open mind about matters scientific, and I'm prepared still to be convinced that one or more of these ideas can work and work well. That said, as the evidence currently stands, I think the intelligent stance regarding debate on these matters is one of extreme skepticism.

Geoengineering Is Really "Geoexperimentation"

First of all, geo-engineering is a lousy term. It implies the certainties of engineering. It makes profound alteration of the Earth's climate and biological systems sound as easy as building a bridge or tunnel or skyscraper, when the reality is that we don't know anywhere near enough about the impacts on systems we're talking about changing to be sure of the results of our meddling. The term "geo-experimentation" or "geo-gambling" might be more accurate.

What's more, geo-experimentation efforts seem to me to be the epitome of carbon blindness [a narrow focus on the problem of carbon dioxide to the exclusion of other threats to the environment]. For instance, it's been pointed out by many other, smarter people that sucking CO_2 [carbon dioxide] into the oceans will worsen ocean acidification, a potential catastrophic ecological problem. So serious is the threat that the IUCN [International Union for Conservation of Nature]'s Kristina M Gjerde recently wrote:

> The oceans are complex, dynamic, unpredictable and already vulnerable to the effects of climate change and acidification. We need mechanisms that will build their resilience, not undermine it. . . . We don't need quick fixes to this global problem that may, in the long-term, cause far more harm than good.

Unintended Consequences Are Likely

Expect similar objections to every proposal for geo-engineering, that doesn't adequately encompass a full understanding of the biological and social consequences, intended or unintended, of intervention. And most of these proposals seem likely to be nothing but huge demonstrations of the law of unintended consequences.

Indeed, the track record of massive-scale environmental interventions is not an encouraging one. From the damming of rivers to fighting forest fires to eliminating pests, our efforts have frequently been revealed in hindsight to be so overrun with unintended consequences as to become full-blown disasters, often disasters worse than the original problems we set out to solve. And, in general, the cost of our errors has tended to increase with the magnitude of the attempted solution. The literature is absolutely chock-a-block [packed] with big failed schemes to control nature.

We already know how to stop climate change, and the downsides of a societal effort to change our land use, adopt clean energy, redesign for energy efficiency and tax waste are minimal, and probably out-weighed by the overall societal benefits. While much innovation remains needed, the challenge, we know, is primarily one of political will.

Governments Cannot Be Trusted to Engineer the Climate

Governments which are incapable of mustering the political will to seriously reduce emissions are not to be trusted to make responsible decisions about mega-engineering projects at a planetary scale. The chances of getting it profoundly wrong—through negligence or greed—are just too great.

And the odds of even a well-intentioned and thoughtful program going profoundly askew are great. In general, the larger the scale of the project, the greater the bureaucratic inertia (in both governments and corporations), the stronger the tendency to corruption and cooked results, and the larger the financial incentives of those involved. Most geo-experimentation schemes would require budgets in the tens or hundreds of billions of dollars. That sort of money tends to make people less willing to admit it when things go wrong . . . and with schemes like these, if things went wrong, they could go wrong in massive and unpredictable ways.

Various Geoengineering Proposals

The following is a schematic representation of various geoengineering and carbon storage proposals.

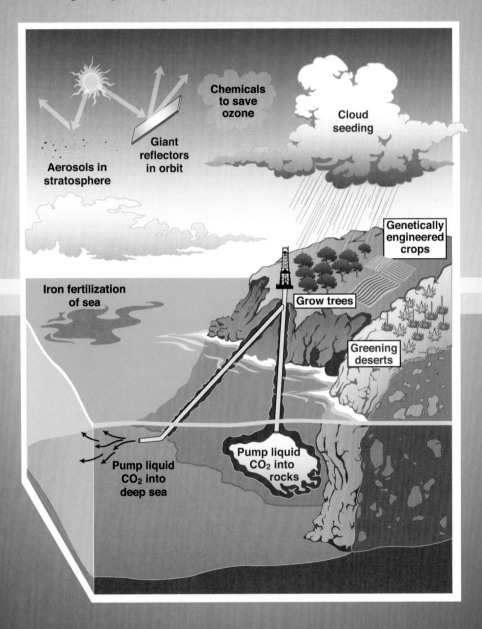

Taken from: Lawrence Livermore National Laboratory, "Geoengineering Could Slow Down the Water Cycle," May 27, 2008.

Geo-experimentation, in practice, might well most closely resemble the U.S. effort to build a national missile defense system [dubbed "Star Wars"] (which has poured tens of billions of dollars down a rat hole of corruption and incompetence, destabilized existing non-proliferation efforts and produced nothing but a long string of failures). Imagine "Star Wars" applied to your climate and the ecosystems upon which you depend.

This is not a matter of being pro- or anti-technology. I'm about as pro-technology as it's possible to get without having tape on my glasses, and I think it's entirely reasonable to make the distinction between smart deployments of technology—tools that are transparent in their agendas, collaborative and democratic in their benefits, and ultimately easy to reverse or modify—and technologies (like nuclear power) which are centralized, secretive, expensive and essentially irreversible. History tells us we ought to respect these with a healthy suspicion, like a snake in the laundry hamper, and assume they're dangerous until they're proven safe.

We don't need geo-engineering. We already have a path forward out of climate chaos. Embracing a bright green future—one which lives within ecological limits and offers real prosperity—is completely within our grasp. Hacking the only planet we've got rather than simply changing the way we live shows a lack of judgment, to put it mildly. Innovation, enterprise and political courage make up a much more realistic plan than attempting some sort of planetary liposuction.

TEN

The Climate Crisis Calls for Christian Spiritual Values

Janet L. Parker

Janet L. Parker is a Christian ethicist and pastor for parish life at Rock Spring Congregational United Church of Christ in Arlington, Virginia. In the following viewpoint Parker contends that while there is much to fear in the rapidly increasing threat of climate change, most environmentalists use an over-reliance on fear to motivate people to take action on climate change. She says the faith community needs to show the world that love is a better motivator. According to Parker, the concept of community must be expanded to include "the entire God-soaked circle of life," so that to love one's neighbor ultimately means to love all life on earth. From this author's perspective, taking action to prevent climate change is a sacred task ultimately motivated by the love of God. She supports her perspective with quotes from the Bible.

Four years have passed since NASA [National Aeronautics and Space Administration] scientist James Hansen sounded this warning: "Multiple lines of evidence indicate that the Earth's climate is nearing . . . a point of no return, beyond which it will be impossible to avoid climate change with far-ranging undesirable consequences."

Janet L. Parker, "Perfect Love Casts Out Fear; Are Scare Tactics the Best Tools in Our Work Against Climate Change?" *Sojourners Magazine*, December 2009, p. 20–23. Copyright © 2009 Sojourners. Reproduced with permission from Sojourners. (800) 714-7474, www.sojo.net.

Increasingly, the chorus coming from the scientific community is harder and harder to drown out—the brutal facts are that we are running out of time. In January 2007, the *Bulletin of the Atomic Scientists* moved its Doomsday Clock two minutes closer to midnight—it now stands at five minutes to midnight—not only because of the ongoing threat of the world's nuclear arsenal, but also the growing threat to all of life posed by climate change.

Climate Change Is Accelerating

The pace of climate change is turning out to be much faster than expected. We seem to be witnessing a perfect storm of triggers. Emissions have gone up faster than expected, leading to more warming. The warming causes the release of carbon from the arctic permafrost, which speeds up the warming, which causes more release from permafrost. As the oceans warm up, the great ice sheets are melting faster, which causes the earth to absorb rather than reflect more of the sun's energy. This reinforces the warming trend. And on top of all this, the increase in wildfires and the destruction of the tropical rainforests releases the carbon stored in millions of trees.

The human and ecological costs of a warming planet stagger the mind. A 2007 Intergovernmental Panel on Climate Change report predicts that 20 to 30 percent of all known species are at increased risk for extinction if the average global temperature rises by more than 2 degrees Celsius from pre-industrial levels. The world's poor will suffer disproportionate effects including loss of critical water and food supplies in Africa and Asia. We are running out of time to avoid a climate catastrophe.

Today, environmentalists do not corner the market on apocalyptic warnings of global collapse. Now the economy competes with climate change and environmental collapse for top billing in our global scare-fest. Job losses, disappearing retirement savings, home foreclosures, and a shattered trust in virtually every financial institution stalk our land like the grim reaper. It's too bad we can't buy stock in fear, because its value would be going through the roof!

Motivating People Through Fear

The question for the faith community is, do we have anything to say to a world that is literally being scared out of its wits?

Often the response of environmentalists, even religious ones, is to fuel the fire and hope that fear will prove to be a better motivator than moral arguments for reducing our carbon footprint and changing public policy. If we can't reason people into making the necessary changes to avert climate catastrophe, maybe we can scare people into them.

There's no denying that fear can be a powerful motivator. We are hard-wired by evolution to respond to the fear impulse. Fear works to lead us into war; it works to condone torture—but at what cost? And is fear ultimately effective in moving us toward our goal of creating a world in which there is enough for all creation?

Relying on fear as our primary ally in galvanizing action on climate change is a dangerous game to play. In human beings, fear can lead to scapegoating, punishing, shaming, and judging. Fear fosters isolation, conflict, and despair. Fear may cause us to take action to protect ourselves and those we love, but it rarely leads to enlightened collective action for the common good.

Love Is a Better Motivator

Fear and love are often mutually exclusive. "There is no fear in love," according to [the Bible's New Testament book of] I John, "but perfect love casts out fear; for fear has to do with punishment, and whoever fears has not reached perfection in love." And here's the rub: If, as Christians believe, the very nature of God is perfect love, and perfect love casts out all fear, then it follows that fear is not of God. And thus we had better be very careful about calling forth the dark energy of fear to combat the specter of climate change.

So what is the alternative? To paraphrase the apostle Paul, is it not the distinctive role of the faith community to show the world a more excellent way?

A few years ago, Michael Shellenberger and Ted Nordhaus decried the special-interest politics and overly technical analyses

Faith-based environmentalists say that emphasizing a love for the environment is a better motivator than the fear tactics some environmentalists use.

used by environmentalists. They wrote: "Martin Luther King Jr.'s 'I have a dream' speech is famous because it put forward an inspiring, positive vision that carried a critique of the current moment within it. Imagine how history would have turned out had King given an 'I have a nightmare' speech instead. . . . The world's most effective leaders . . . distinguish themselves by inspiring hope against fear, love against injustice, and power against powerlessness."

"Environmentalists," they continued, "need to tap into the creative worlds of myth-making, even religion, not to better sell narrow and technical policy proposals but rather to figure out who we are and who we need to be."

The way forward, I would propose, is to rediscover and resituate the two great commandments of Jesus in an ecological context—a context that widens our moral community to include the entire God-soaked circle of life.

Jesus links these two commandments together, as the summation of the entire law and prophets, for the very substance of the love of God is given shape and form as we love our neighbor as ourselves. But, with the lawyer in the gospel of Luke, it's time to ask for a bit of clarification on this point. What we need desperately to understand is who our neighbor is and how we are to love God in our neighbor. Jesus' answer to these questions was radical—blowing wide open the assumptions about who should fall within our circle of concern. For Jesus, our neighbor was the outcast, the scapegoat, the stranger, the sinner, the criminal, the homeless and hungry poor, and even the enemy. To fulfill the spirit of Jesus' commandments today, even the species boundary must be crossed.

A Progressive Christian Spirituality Honors Nature

"A Christian spirituality insists that we work out right relations with God and neighbor," wrote Sallie McFague in *Super, Natural Christians*. "It should include right relations with creation as well. . . . Nature is certainly among the poor and oppressed in our time. Our right relations with nature should therefore be guided by Jesus' praxis [formal practice]."

This ecological Christian understanding of neighbor-love cannot fall prey to the temptations that ensnare some environmentalists, who seek to preserve "nature" without regard to the needs of the human beings who live in it. In fact, a Christian environmentalism will focus on the places where the neediest human

"Ecology" cartoon by Ronaldo Dias. www.CartoonStock.com.

beings and the neediest parts of nature meet. And we will do so in partnership with, not in condescension to, those whom we seek to serve.

"Part of adopting an attitude of love when we do our work on climate change," wrote Noelle Damico of the Coalition of Immokalee

Workers, "means taking the time it takes to work together with the organized poor who have been most affected by issues of climate change. . . . It means taking our cue from what our sisters and brothers who have been made poor are doing, how they are resisting, and how we can pair up our power and our efforts with theirs."

Protecting the Environment Is Sacred Work

The holy work of the mystic and the holy work of the activist is thus the same. It is the work of love—love for God, love for each creature that dwells in the heart of God, love that trembles with compassion at suffering and swells with anger over injustice.

The brilliance of this spiritual path to which we are called is that the energy to love our neighbor and to strive to repair our world arises naturally within us when we are connected to our divine Source.

Here we see why love is superior to fear. Fear motivates us for a moment, but when the immediate perception of the threat is passed, it subsides. Love is inexhaustible, flowing from the very heart of God. Fear can lead to paralysis and despair as often as it leads to action. Love gives us the strength to continue to fight for what we love, and to make great personal sacrifices for the sake of our beloved. Fear may cause us to relocate our family away from a coastline threatened by rising seas, but love calls us to address the causes of climate change and to provide support for those most vulnerable to its impact, so that every family is protected.

This is our vision—a beloved creation of raucous diversity and extravagant beauty, a web of life knit together by the Spirit of God who infuses every cell. It is a deeply religious vision, and yet it can easily be translated into the language of the public sphere. Doing justice, promoting equity, ensuring freedom, and conserving nature are the social dimensions of loving our neighbor as ourselves.

As we go about this holy work, we are sustained by the loving presence of the God who is closer than our breath. If we grow weary, we can take comfort in Jesus' promise, "Where two or three are gathered in my name, I am there among you."

ELEVEN

A Catastrophe Is Needed to Spur Action on Climate Change

Eric Reguly

Eric Reguly is an award-winning Canadian newspaper columnist writing for the *Globe and Mail*, a major Toronto, Ontario paper. In the following viewpoint, Reguly says that despite many statements by leaders about how serious climate change is, those statements were not enough to produce a binding treaty or create a plan of action to prevent climate change at the United Nations Climate Change Conference in Copenhagen, Denmark, in 2009. According to Reguly, no substantial action has been taken because the climate change crisis has not had a highly visible disaster that would spur leaders and citizens to take the drastic action that is needed. He argues that while the terrorist attacks by al Qaeda on September 11, 2001 caused the United States to launch two wars, and the financial crisis in 2008 triggered a massive response by the government, no similarly spectacular crisis has yet occurred due to climate change. The author claims that such a large-scale crisis could happen at any time, but by then it may be too late to do much about it.

Every leader [at the 2009 United Nations Climate Change Conference in Copenhagen] said the same thing. The climate change science is real. The need to act now is urgent. The end is nigh. "Hurricanes, floods, typhoons and droughts that were once all regarded as the acts of an invisible God are now revealed to be the visible acts of man," Britain's [prime minister] Gordon Brown said.

"We come here in Copenhagen because climate change poses a grave and growing danger to our people," [then U.S. senator and now president] Barack Obama said. A weak climate change deal would be "an invitation to Africa to sign a suicide pact," the Sudanese ambassador said.

And so on, times 193 countries. And then nothing.

The Copenhagen Accord, reached after two weeks of round-the-clock negotiations, produced no binding treaty, no specific emissions-reduction targets, no plan for a carbon market, no sense of where the money for the promised $30-billion (U.S.) climate change fund would come from or where it would be spent.

A climate change catastrophe, such as the El Nino's periodic warming of the Pacific Ocean, could cause widespread flooding and extreme drought conditions in the western United States.

Everyone went home while the debris from the conference to prevent the planet from baking was cleared away to make room for a design and accessories show to take over the conference centre.

Not Very Noticeable Yet

How do you explain the huge gap between the rhetoric and the outcome? There were dozens of theories, each credible to some degree. Certainly there was a rift between the leaders and their negotiators. The former begged for action; the latter drowned in an ocean of mistrust. They had seen it all before, starting in 1992 at the Rio de Janeiro Earth Summit, when the industrialized countries promised to rein in greenhouse-gas emissions and help the poor countries adapt their economies and societies to a warming planet. Seventeen years of broken promises meant the negotiators arrived in Copenhagen with little hope that the climate-change meeting—the 15th—would be different.

But maybe the summit failed because there was no clear and present danger, at least one you could see. Carbon dioxide is a clear, odourless gas. Each human is a small carbon dioxide factory. Yes the Arctic, Greenland and Antarctic ice fields are melting in Al Gore's videos. Britain's national weather service said the current decade had the highest global temperatures on record. Just don't ask us to get worried about the Big Melt when no one we know is dying from it.

Copenhagen's dud status shows that perverse disaster psychology is alive and well—no disaster meant no action. That's unlikely to change until the climate change story has its Pearl Harbor moment, an event so catastrophic, so violent, that it instantly mobilizes entire countries. By then, of course, it may be too late.

People React Quickly When Disasters Strike

The Japanese attack on Pearl Harbor [a U.S. naval base in Hawaii] on Dec. 7, 1941, immediately put the United States on war footing. The economy and society were transformed virtually overnight. Detroit's car factories pumped out tanks and bombers.

Millions of women worked the armaments lines while their men went to war in the Pacific and in Europe.

A similar scenario unfolded after the terrorist attacks of Sept. 11, 2001. Two wars were launched. Last year [2008], the financial crisis and the recession triggered bank bailouts, stimulus spending and liquidity injections valued at trillions of dollars around the world. April's G20 summit in London [where the top 20 global economic powers met] showed that countries can move with alacrity to fight a common threat.

What could climate change's Pearl Harbor look like? If you read the literature from the Woods Hole Oceanographic Institution, it could be a sudden shift in the ocean currents—known as the ocean conveyor—that transport warm water from the Southern Hemisphere to the Northern Hemisphere. It might be extreme bouts of El Niño (the periodic warming of Pacific Ocean surface temperatures), or La Niña (Pacific cooling), either of which could trigger extreme floods, droughts and other forms of extreme as they have in the past.

Catastrophe Could Happen at Any Time

It might be a massive African or Asian drought that wipes out crops across several countries. The Australian drought in 2009, where rainfall in some parts of [the] country was a mere 5 per cent to 10 per cent of historical totals, gave us a hint of the agricultural and economic devastation that one dry year can produce. Imagine the same weather pattern in a poor, densely populated country such as Pakistan. Josette Sheeran, the executive director of United Nations World Food Program, the world's biggest humanitarian agency, said hungry people do one of three things: "They riot, they migrate or they die."

The opening lines of the Copenhagen Accord read: "We underline that climate change is one of the greatest challenges of our time. We emphasize our strong political will to urgently combat climate change."

Imagine if the lines went this way instead: "We underline that Al-Qaeda is one of the greatest challenges of our time. . . ." Or substitute "climate change" for "financial crisis" for similar effect.

The words "climate change" simply don't trigger collective fear, at least in the rich world, which thinks it can overcome any problem by throwing money at it. Until an environmental Pearl Harbor happens, climate change is likely to stay on the political and economic security sidelines. Copenhagen showed that. Some 120 leaders pleaded for "urgent" action and the message was lost for want of a horrific, body-strewn, image to go with it.

TWELVE

Young People Can Take Action to Address Climate Change

Peg Cornell

In the following viewpoint, written to a youthful audience, Peg Cornell states that young people did not create climate change and other global problems, but nevertheless they will have to deal with them. The author suggests that to effectively address these problems, young people need to take the following actions: (1) communicate with compassion; (2) act from hope, rather than despair; (3) take action to create changes in the world. She argues that the choices people make in how they spend money can have a huge impact on the environment, suggesting that "spending money on an item is the same as voting in support of all the practices that went into producing it." Peg Cornell is a science teacher in Corvallis, Oregon.

During the 20 years that I have been a high school science teacher, I have watched environmental degradation and global inequities become more severe. The planet is at risk because of our actions.

You didn't cause climate change, species extinctions and other global problems, you are inheriting them from my generation and those before me, but you still must share in the responsibility of solving them. You are flexible thinkers, you are smart and

Peg Cornell, "Live by Design, Not by Default," *Skipping Stones*, vol. 21, September–October, 2009, p. 3+. Copyright © 2009 Stepping Stones. Reproduced by permission.

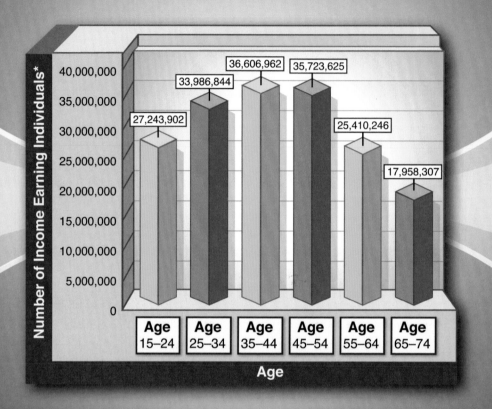

Number of Income Earning Individuals by Age Group for 2005

Number of Income Earning Individuals*

40,000,000		36,606,962	35,723,625
35,000,000	33,986,844		
30,000,000			25,410,246
27,243,902			
25,000,000			17,958,307
20,000,000			
15,000,000			
10,000,000			
5,000,000			
0			

| Age 15–24 | Age 25–34 | Age 35–44 | Age 45–54 | Age 55–64 | Age 65–74 |

Age

*For Income Range Between $0 and $95,000 (Constant 2004 USD)

Taken from: "Income/Age Demographic Snapshots of 1995 and 2005," Political Calculations, May 30, 2007.

creative, you are passionate and have a lot of energy—we need what you have to offer in order to fix the mess our planet is in.

To be an effective advocate for sustainability, I believe there are three guiding practices that should be followed: compassionate communication, hope, and action. These three practices are contrary to the more common practices of violent communication, despair, and apathy. I challenge you today to live your life in a humane and ecologically friendly manner, which will sometimes mean acting in ways radically different from those of your peers. These practices are not always easy, but they are worth the effort.

Communicate with Compassion

The first guiding practice is compassionate communication. In any conversation about environmental or social justice issues, there are usually controversial topics that come up. These topics are often emotional, and if there are disagreements, the conversation can easily become a shouting match. It is important to always have compassion for the person with whom you are speaking, no matter how much you might disagree, and to practice positive communication strategies for sharing difficult information. Unfortunately, you rarely observe people in disagreement use conversation that leads to real understanding and growth. You mostly see what is often called "violent communication," where the purpose is not learning, but rather being "right"—or at least being the loudest and hopefully having the last word. Avoid this approach. You want people to hear what you have to say, and you need to hear and understand their perspective as well. If the way you communicate prevents people from hearing your message, re-evaluate your delivery style. In other words, don't let how you deliver your message get in the way of what your message is about.

Also, remember that not all communication is verbal. Don't underestimate the importance of modeling compassion and sustainable practices in your everyday life. It is critical to "walk the talk." I'm sure all of you can think of someone who speaks about an issue in one way, but then acts in a way completely opposite. Don't be that person! To paraphrase the timeless words of [twentieth-century Indian political activist and spiritual leader] Mahatma Gandhi, "Let your life be your message." If you truly revere and respect the Earth and all her inhabitants, and if you want others to do the same, have compassion even for those with whom you disagree, and let your words and actions be consistent.

Hope Is a Better Motivator than Despair

The second guiding practice is hope. With all the bad news about the environment, it is far too easy to fall into despair. Do any of you ever feel despair when thinking about the state of our world? I certainly do, and I have to stay vigilant to avoid it.

The Cycle of Despair goes something like this.

1. You find out about a problem, and you want to do something to help.
2. You don't see how you can help so you don't do anything about it.
3. You feel sad, powerless, and angry. You decide nothing can be done, so you want to know less and less about problems.

These steps take no effort, which is why so many people end up in this cycle. However, the cycle of despair just leads to indifference and inaction, with no chance for the positive change we need. In the words of [nineteenth-century education reformer] Horace Mann, "A different world cannot be built by indifferent people." We need a different world, so practice the cycle of hope. I have to warn you that hope isn't always easy. Hope takes work, and it takes effort!

But hope is worth it.

Here is the Cycle of Hope.

Step 1. You take personal responsibility for your choices. This means you pay attention to the choices you make—even the small ones—and acknowledge they are your choices and no one else's.

Step 2. You seek quality information about the world's problems, you think critically to distinguish between accurate and inaccurate information, and you analyze sources for validity. There is a lot of false information out there; you must determine what is fact and what is not. Being a critical thinker is not just important at school, it's absolutely necessary in the real world. Don't be fooled by pseudoscience or the media that claim to have the truth without the data to back it up.

Step 3. You create a vision of a better world based on accurate information, your values, and your sense of responsibility; you discover practical options for action; you act in line with your values; and you understand the impact your actions have on the planet.

Strong Action Is Needed to Save the Planet

As you can see, if you practice hope, you naturally reach the third practice, of taking action. I applaud those of you who choose to make a difference by your efforts, but I must tell you that the planet needs more from you—it needs more from all of us. I heard a couple of scientists on the radio recently, and one of them said, "The environment is not a luxury item." Well, duh! But we all know people who treat the environment exactly that way. We in this country are especially hard on the earth. If everyone lived like we do here in the United States, we would need four more planets to support them. We don't have four more planets! We need to change our perception of the environment from something we can change when it is convenient for us, to an issue we must act on now.

A lot of people think the only worthwhile actions involve spending a lot of money to buy solar panels or a hybrid car. As it turns out, you can have a very positive impact on the planet by buying less stuff. Remember the phrase "reduce, reuse, recycle" begins with reduce. Buying less stuff is a really earth-friendly thing to do. And if you do buy something, you can still make a positive difference by choosing carefully. Every time you buy something, whether you realize it or not, you are voting. Spending money on an item is the same as voting in support of all the practices that went into producing it. You are supporting the way the workers were treated, the way the environment was treated, and the way animals and other species were treated. As a young consumer, you have a lot of voting power; in 2004 alone, teens (aged 12–17) spent more than $124 billion, which is close to what adults between the ages of 40 and 58 spent. That is a lot of spending and a lot of voting. You need to know what you are voting for. Money can be an effective tool to facilitate change, and companies do pay attention to consumer expectations and will change their practices. Here's just one example.

Spending Money Wisely Helps the Environment

I'm sure most of you like ice cream and are familiar with Tillamook ice cream. A few years ago, Tillamook Farms [in Oregon] fed their cows bovine growth hormone (BGH) that made the cows produce more milk, which increased Tillamook's profits. And more milk means more ice cream. Yum! Well, as it turns out, not so yum, because BGH was bad for cows' health and potentially bad for human health as well. Understandably, consumers wanted ice cream that didn't hurt cows or people, so they stopped buying Tillamook ice cream. What do you think happened? Tillamook stopped feeding their cows BGH and consumers began buying their ice cream again. That is the power of the consumer vote.

The author agrees with American anthropologist Margaret Mead (pictured), who said, "Never doubt that a small group of thoughtful, committed citizens can change the world. Indeed it is the only thing that ever has."

So, research where the stuff you buy comes from and how it was made, everything from the food you eat to the clothes you wear. Become an informed consumer and only purchase items made in an ecologically friendly way—that is, in a way that is friendly to the workers, to the local population and to the environment. Other actions are up to you!

I'd like to share three quotes I reflect on every day before I teach. They inspire me and give me hope even when I feel like things will never get better.

The first quote might be familiar to most, if not, all of you, a classic from Gandhi: "Be the change you want to see in the world."

The second quote is more obscure, but it's my favorite. It is from Richard Bach, who is best known for his book, *Jonathan Livingston Seagull*: "Argue for your limitations, and sure enough, they're yours."

Lastly, one from [twentieth-century anthropologist] Margaret Mead: "Never doubt that a small group of thoughtful, committed citizens can change the world. Indeed, it is the only thing that ever has."

I challenge you today to be the change you hope to see, to argue not for your limitations, but for your possibilities, and to consider yourselves to be the small group that can change the world.

What You Should Know About Climate Change

Historical and Observed Effects of Climate Change

According to the Intergovernmental Panel on Climate Change (IPCC), as of 2007,

- The world's surface air temperature increased an average of 1 degree Fahrenheit during the twentieth century.
- Global warming has occurred in phases, with the rate of warming increasing over time: From the 1910s to the 1940s there was an overall increase of 0.63 degrees Fahrenheit, whereas from the 1970s to 2007 the temperature increased 1 degree Fahrenheit.
- Eleven of the twelve warmest years ever recorded have occurred in the past twelve years.
- During the twentieth century, the estimated water vapor content of the atmosphere increased by 5 percent, because warmer air has a greater water-holding capacity, increasing the risk of both drought and flooding.
- In the summer of 2002 Europe experienced widespread flooding, followed in 2003 by record-breaking heat waves and drought.
- Since 1970 category four and five hurricanes have increased by 75 percent.
- In the Northern Hemisphere, since 1966 spring snow cover has decreased by 2 percent per decade.

- During the twentieth century average global sea levels increased by about 0.07 inches per year, after remaining stable for the previous two thousand years.
- Recently, average global sea levels have been rising at an accelerated pace; since 1993 it has increased by about 0.12 inches per year.
- Until recently, atmospheric carbon dioxide (CO_2) levels have never increased by more than thirty parts per million (ppm) per one thousand years. However, since 1993 atmospheric CO_2 levels have increased by thirty ppm.

The U.S. Global Change Research Program, in a comprehensive report titled *Global Climate Change Impacts in the United States*, released in June 2009, reports that

- As of 2008, atmospheric CO_2 levels are 385 ppm, 30 percent greater than the highest levels reached in the last eight hundred thousand years.
- CO_2 is being released at an accelerating rate: In the 1990s atmospheric CO_2 increased by 1.3 percent per year; between 2000 and 2006 it increased by 3.3 percent per year.
- Over the last century global sea levels have risen by eight inches, and in the past fifteen years the rate of increase has doubled.
- In some U.S. coastal areas, sea levels have increased by eight inches or more in the past fifty years.
- Over the past fifty years, average temperature in the United States has increased by more than 2 degrees Fahrenheit.
- In the past thirty years, winter temperatures have increased more than any other season, in some regions rising by more than 7 degrees Fahrenheit.
- The risk of a heat wave such as the one that occurred in Europe in 2003 is now about four times greater than would have been the case without human-caused climate change.
- Precipitation in the United States has increased by around 5 percent in the past fifty years.

- In the past century in the United States, overall levels of precipitation have increased by about 7 percent, while rainfall in the heaviest downpours has risen by an average of about 20 percent.
- Over the past several decades, end-of-summer Arctic sea ice has declined by over 11 percent per decade, reaching a record low in 2007.
- Unexpected occurrences due to climate change have been observed. For example, increased carbon dioxide in the atmosphere has recently been shown to be making oceans more acidic, harming coral and other sea life.

According to the National Oceanic and Atmospheric Administration's *State of the Climate Global Analysis June 2010* report,
- June 2010 set a record for the highest combined global land and ocean average surface temperature yet recorded; at 61.1 degrees Fahrenheit, it was 1.22 degrees Fahrenheit higher than the twentieth-century average.
- June 2010 was the 304th consecutive month with a global temperature higher than the twentieth-century average, and was the fourth month in a row to set a record temperature.
- The last month that had a below-average temperature was February 1985.
- The global average land surface temperature in June 2010 was 1.93 degrees Fahrenheit higher than the twentieth-century average and is the warmest yet recorded.

According to the World Health Organization, reporting in January 2010,
- As of 2004, effects due to climate change have caused more than 140,000 excess deaths per year since the 1970s.
- Global warming is causing more frequent and extreme heat waves. In the summer of 2003 more than 70,000 excess deaths occurred due to a heat wave in Europe.

- Weather-related natural disasters have more than tripled since the 1960s; such disasters kill over sixty thousand people per year, mostly in developing countries.

The National Aeronautics and Space Administration (NASA) Goddard Institute for Space Studies reported in January 2010 that

- The year 2009 was tied with 1998, 2002, 2003, 2006 and 2007 as the second-warmest year since records began in 1880, and was only slightly cooler than the warmest year on record (2005).
- The warmest decade thus far recorded is January 2000 to December 2009.
- Surface temperature has increased by 0.36 degrees Farenheit each decade for the past three decades.
- Since 1880, average global temperatures have risen by about 1.5 degrees Farenheit.

Projected Impacts of Climate Change

The U.S. Global Change Research Program, in a comprehensive report released in June 2009, reports that

- By 2100, average global temperature is projected to increase by anywhere from 2 degrees Fahrenheit (if greenhouse gas emissions are cut substantially) to 11.5 degrees Fahrenheit if emissions continue on their current trajectory.
- Research suggests that a further increase of 2 degrees Fahrenheit over present levels would have severe and irreversible impacts over much of the earth.
- U.S. average temperature is likely to increase more than the global average over the twenty-first century, with regional variations.
- As climate change continues, both droughts and flooding will occur more frequently and be more extreme, due to the increased water vapor holding capacity of the warmer atmosphere.
- If emissions continue to increase, recent studies suggest sea levels will likely rise by three to four feet by the end of the twenty-first century.

- Most of the United States is expected to experience more warming in summer than winter, except for Alaska, which will experience warmer winters.
- In higher-emissions scenarios, extreme weather events that now happen about once every twenty years are expected to happen every other year, and very hot days will be 10 degrees Fahrenheit hotter than they are now.
- Assuming greenhouse gas emissions keep rising, by the middle of the twenty-first century European summers will be hotter than the extreme heat wave of 2003, and by the end of the century the summer of 2003 would be considered unusually cool in comparison.
- Climate change puts much coastal roadway at risk. In the U.S. Gulf Coast area alone, an expanse of twenty-four hundred miles of major roadway is expected to be permanently flooded due to rising sea levels over the next fifty to one hundred years.
- Declining sea ice in the Arctic will provide great opportunities for shippers, likely including new ice-free ports and longer shipping seasons, as well as access to a new Northwest Passage sometime during this century.
- By the middle of the century the global polar bear population is expected to be reduced by two-thirds; in Alaska it is expected that wild polar bears will have disappeared completely within seventy-five years.

The Intergovernmental Panel on Climate Change (IPCC) reports as of 2007 that
- Over the next twenty years, global average temperature is expected to increase by 0.36 degrees Fahrenheit per decade.
- Under a low greenhouse-gas emissions scenario, the global average temperature will increase by 3.2 degrees Fahrenheit over the twenty-first century; under a high-emissions scenario the temperature will increase 7.2 degrees Fahrenheit.
- The range considered likely to occur is from 2 degrees Fahrenheit for a low-emissions scenario to a maximum of 11.5 degrees Fahrenheit for a high-emissions scenario.

- By the end of the twenty-first century, sea levels could rise anywhere from 7.2 inches to 23.6 inches under various emissions scenarios.
- Even if greenhouse gas concentrations are stabilized at current levels, human-caused global warming and rise in sea levels are expected to increase for centuries.
- Extreme weather events such as heat waves and heavy precipitation are considered very likely to occur more often throughout the twenty-first century.
- Under all emissions scenarios considered likely, CO_2 concentration in the atmosphere by the year 2100 is expected to range from 535 to 983 ppm.
- Warming will occur unevenly around the world, with land areas warming more than oceans and temperatures at high latitudes increasing more than those at low latitudes.
- It is considered unlikely but possible that the West Antarctic Ice Sheet could slide into the ocean over the next few centuries if global warming continues; if so, sea levels would rise by seventeen to twenty feet.

The World Health Organization reported in January 2010 that
- By the last decade of the twenty-first century, extreme drought is expected to double in frequency and last six times as long on average.
- Staple foods in many extremely poor areas of the world will decline dramatically due to rising temperatures and changing precipitation patterns; in some African countries the supply of staple foods may be cut in half by 2020.
- Climate change will likely lengthen the range and transmission seasons of many deadly disease vectors, such as insects— for example, the range of dengue fever–bearing mosquitoes may expand to put an additional 2 billion people at risk of that deadly disease by the 2080s.

What You Should Do About Climate Change

Gather Information

The first step in grappling with any complex and controversial issue is to be informed about it. Gather as much information as you can from a variety of sources. The essays in this book form an excellent starting point, representing a variety of viewpoints and approaches to the topic of climate change. Your school or local library will be another source of useful information; look there for relevant books, magazines, and encyclopedia entries. The bibliography and organizations to contact sections of this book provide relevant sources for gathering additional information.

The last several decades have seen an enormous increase in the amount of information available on climate change. Many scientific articles and reports on all aspects of this important issue have been published. If the information in such articles is too dense or technical to comprehend, read the abstract at the beginning of an article, which provides a clear summary of the researcher's conclusions.

Internet search engines will be helpful to you in your research. There are many blogs and Web sites that cover climate change from a variety of perspectives, including concerned individuals offering their opinions and advice, advocacy organizations, popular media outlets, and governmental and scientific organizations. Be aware that not all online sources are equally valid or reliable.

Identify the Issues Involved

Once you have gathered your information, review it methodically to discover the key issues involved. What evidence is there that the climate has already begun to change? How might the climate change in the future? What theories do people have about the causes of climate change and are such changes caused by natural variations or human activity, or a combination of both? How serious a threat might climate change pose to humanity and the rest of the natural world, and what—if anything—can be done about it? What solutions are proposed for dealing with the problem, and what are the possible consequences of various strategies for dealing with climate change? How has scientific opinion on the issue changed over time?

Notice that although the issue is often presented by the mainstream media in a two-sided manner, there are actually many perspectives to consider. For example, the skeptical position includes those who don't believe climate change is happening at all, those who believe it's happening but it's not an urgent problem, those who believe the climate is changing but that it is mainly due to natural causes rather than to human activity, and so on. Conversely, among people who consider climate change an imminent threat to humanity, there are those who feel all efforts should be made to slow down, or mitigate, climate change and those who believe it is too late to do anything to stop the process and therefore the best strategy is to put all efforts into adapting to climate changes. Even those who advocate adaptation or mitigation offer many different opinions on how best to pursue those strategies.

Evaluate Your Information Sources

In developing your own opinion, it is vital to evaluate the sources of the information you have discovered. Authors of books, magazine articles, and so forth, however well intentioned, have their own perspectives and biases that may affect how they present information on the subject. This is particularly true of a highly charged issue like climate change, where some of the possible scenarios put the very survival of the human species at risk, and billions or even trillions of dollars are at stake, depending on the nature of the climate crisis and how the world responds to it.

Consider the authors' credentials and organizational affiliations. They may offer information that is perfectly valid, but may skew data that supports their viewpoint or the viewpoint of their affiliated organizations; for example, someone who is affiliated with a major oil company is likely to promote information and ideas that support the continuing use of fossil fuels. Someone who is affiliated with a solar power company may argue that solar power is the only safe energy source and present information and perspectives arguing in favor of solar and against any alternatives. On the other hand, if you find someone arguing against his or her expected bias—for example, an oil executive arguing for a drastic reduction in fossil fuel use, or an environmental organization that had long opposed nuclear power pushing for more nuclear plants to reduce carbon dioxide emissions—it may be worthwhile to pay particular attention to what is being said. Always critically evaluate and assess your sources rather than take whatever they say at face value.

Examine Your Own Perspective

Consider your own beliefs, feelings, and biases on this subject. Perhaps you have been influenced by the attitudes of family or friends or by media reports. If you had a position on climate change before reading this book, think about whether anything you have now read has made you reconsider your opinions. Seek out and contemplate information and perspectives that differ from what you already believe to be true. Be aware of the common tendency to look for evidence that confirms what you already believe to be true and to discount anything that contradicts your viewpoint.

Form Your Own Opinion

Once you have gathered and organized information, identified the issues involved, and examined your own perspective, you will be ready to form an opinion on climate change and to advocate that position in debates and discussions. You may conclude that climate change is a dire threat to humanity that requires decisive action, in which case you might advocate mitigation or adaptation strategies, or you may decide that the threat is exaggerated. You may discover useful common ground between conflicting positions, particularly in terms of suggested courses of action. For example, some argue that people should drive less to reduce the carbon dioxide produced by burning fossil fuels such as gasoline. Others believe that climate change and carbon dioxide emissions are not a problem—but they might agree that driving less is a good way to reduce America's dependence on foreign oil and that walking and bicycling are pleasant sources of healthy exercise. Whatever position you take, be prepared to explain it clearly based on facts, evidence, and well-thought-out ideas.

Take Action

There is much that can be done by individuals to address climate change. Advocating your position in discussions and debates is one means of achieving change. Another possibility would be to join an activist organization that shares your beliefs about climate change—check out the Organizations to Contact section of this book for some starting points. Perhaps your school or community has an environmental club or organization; if not, you may decide to form one yourself. If you would like to contact your political representatives directly to express your position on climate change and what you think should be done about it, the Web site www.usa.gov/Contact/Elected.shtml can help you get started.

If you would like to reduce your greenhouse gas emissions there are many ways to do so. Walking, cycling, and taking public transit are the most environmentally friendly modes of transportation. Buying local food can save the greenhouse gas emissions that can result from transporting food long distances. Using energy more efficiently reduces the amount of carbon dioxide released from fossil-fuel-burning power plants. For example, compact fluorescent light bulbs consume up to 75 percent less electricity than conventional, incandescent bulbs. More than half of the energy used in a home in the United States comes from heating and air conditioning, so reducing the use of those can save a lot of energy and reduce CO_2 emissions. The U.S. Environmental Protection Agency has additional ideas and resources for reducing greenhouse gas emissions; visit its Web site at www.epa.gov/climate change/wycd/index.html for more information.

The editors have compiled the following list of organizations concerned with the issues debated in this book. The descriptions are derived from materials provided by the organizations. All have publications or information available for interested readers. The list was compiled on the date of publication of the present volume; the information provided here may change. Be aware that many organizations take several weeks or longer to respond to inquiries, so allow as much time as possible for the receipt of requested materials.

The Alliance for Climate Protection
PO Box 1332
Menlo Park, CA 94026
(650) 543-7395
e-mail: ravi.garla@climateprotect.org
website: www.climateprotect.org

The Alliance for Climate Protection's purpose is to persuade people of the importance, urgency, and feasibility of adopting and implementing effective and comprehensive solutions for the climate crisis. It advocates nonpartisan alliances, uses innovative and far-reaching communication techniques, and has created the We campaign (www.wecansolveit.org) to further its goal.

Climate Solutions
1402 Third Ave., Suite 1305
Seattle, WA 98101
(206) 443-9570
e-mail: info@climatesolutions.org
website: www.climatesolutions.org

Climate Solutions, a nonprofit organization located in the Pacific Northwest, was formed in 1998 to develop ways to act decisively and creatively toward addressing the global warming crisis. Its website contains background information on global warming, discusses solutions, and provides a variety of publications on the subject.

Friends of Science (FOS)
PO Box 23167, Connaught Post Office
Calgary, AB T2S 3B1 Canada
e-mail: contact@friendsofscience.org
website: www.friendsofscience.org/

FOS conducts literature research and draws on the body of work by scientists in all fields relating to global climate change. It takes the position that the sun is the main direct and indirect driver of climate change. The website provides extensive written, audio, and video materials supporting its view and critiquing the mainstream consensus on climate change.

Global Warming International Center
PO Box 50303, Palo Alto, CA
(630) 910-1551
fax: (630) 910-1561
website: www.globalwarming.net

The Global Warming International Center disseminates information on global warming science and policy and sponsors research to further the understanding and mitigation of global warming. News releases, press statements, and a variety of papers on global warming can be found on the group's website.

Hudson Institute
1015 Fifteenth St. NW, Fl. 6
Washington, DC 20005
(202) 974-2400
fax: (202) 974-2410
e-mail: info@hudson.org
website: www.hudson.org

The Hudson Institute is a nonpartisan policy research organization dedicated to research and analysis aimed at promoting global security, prosperity, and freedom. A search of the group's website produces a list of articles and commentaries on issues relating to climate change, many of which are critical of mainstream advocacy.

International Climate Science Coalition (ICSC)
PO Box 23013
Ottawa, ON K2A 4E2 Canada
(613) 728-9200
website: www.climatescienceinternational.org/

The ICSC is an association of independent scientists, economists, and energy and policy experts. Its stated aim is to support a more rational, open discussion about climate issues to move the debate away from implementation of what it sees as costly and ineffective climate control measures. It holds the view that human activity is not causing dangerous climate change and that no consensus to that effect exists among scientists.

National Council for Science and the Environment (NCSE)
1101 Seventeenth St. NW, Suite 250
Washington, DC 20036
(202) 530-5810
e-mail: info@ncseonline.org
website: http://ncseonline.org/

NCSE is a not-for-profit organization dedicated to improving everyone's understanding of the scientific basis for environmental decision making by fostering collaboration among institutions, communities, and individuals. It offers the Encyclopedia of Earth (www.eoearth.org/), an electronic reference about the earth, its natural environments, and its interaction with society. The encyclopedia is a free collection of articles written in nontechnical language by scholars, professionals, educators, and experts who collaborate and review each other's work.

Natural Resources Defense Council (NRDC)
40 W. Twentieth St., New York, NY 10011
(212) 727-2700
fax: (212) 727-1773
e-mail: nrdcinfo@nrdc.org
website: www.nrdc.org/globalwarming

The NRDC is an environmental organization that uses law, science, and the support of 1.3 million members and online activists to protect the planet's wildlife and wild places and to ensure a safe and healthy environment for all living things. The NRDC website contains a special section on global warming that provides many articles and reports on the issue.

Pew Center on Global Climate Change
2101 Wilson Blvd., Suite 550, Arlington, VA 22201
(703) 516-4146
fax: (703) 841-1422
website: www.pewclimate.org

The Pew Center on Global Climate Change is a nonprofit, independent organization founded to provide credible information and solutions on climate change. The center brings together business leaders, policy makers, scientists, and other experts to formulate a new approach to a complex and often controversial issue. The group's website provides both basic and in-depth information and fact sheets on climate change, as well as access to Pew Center reports and links to a variety of other relevant materials.

Reason Foundation
3415 S. Sepulveda Blvd., Suite 400
Los Angeles, CA 90034
(310) 391-2245
fax: (310) 391-4395
website: www.reason.org

The Reason Foundation is a national public policy research organization that promotes libertarian principles, including individual liberty, free markets, and the rule of law. The foundation publishes the monthly magazine *Reason*, and a search of its website for "climate change" produces a long list of articles and commentaries on this topic.

350.org
(510) 250-7860
website: www.350.org/

The 350.org is an international campaign working to build a movement to unite the world around solutions to the climate crisis. It aims to get the global atmosphere below 350 parts per million (ppm) of carbon dioxide (CO_2), which it claims is the highest safe level in terms of the greenhouse effect. Evidence supporting this claim is provided on its website as well as many ideas on what can be done to achieve this goal.

Union of Concerned Scientists (UCS)
2 Brattle Sq., Cambridge, MA 02238-9105
(617) 547-5552
fax: (617) 864-9405
website: www.ucsusa.org

The UCS is a science-based nonprofit organization that works to create a healthy environment and a safer world. Using independent scientific research and citizen action, UCS proposes solutions to environmental problems and works to secure necessary changes in government policy, corporate practices, and consumer choices. The UCS website contains a highly informative section on global warming, including information on the science behind the phenomenon and possible solutions.

United Nations Framework Convention on Climate Change (UNFCCC)
PO Box 260124, Bonn D-53153 Germany
+49 228 815-1000
fax: +49 228 815-1999
e-mail: secretariat@unfccc.int
website: http://unfccc.int

The UNFCCC is the first international treaty on climate change. This United Nations website offers information about this and subsequent treaties such as the Kyoto Protocol and the Copenhagen Accord. It offers the UNFCCC E-Newsletter, which provides an overview of major news and announcements on climate change issues.

United Nations Intergovernmental Panel on Climate Change (IPCC)
IPCC Secretariat, c/o World Meteorological Organization
7bis Ave. de la Paix, CP 2300, Geneva 2 CH-1211 Switzerland
+41 22 730-8208
fax: +41 22 730-8025
e-mail: ipcc-sec@wmo.int
website: www.ipcc.ch/

The IPCC was established by the United Nations Environment Programme and the World Meteorological Organization in 1988 to assess the scientific, technical, and socioeconomic information relating to human-induced climate change, its potential impacts, and possible solutions. The IPCC website is a source for authoritative assessment reports, technical papers, and other publications.

U.S. Environmental Protection Agency (EPA)
Climate Change Division
Ariel Rios Bldg., 1200 Pennsylvania Ave. NW
Washington, DC 20460
(202) 343-9990
e-mail: climatechange@epa.gov
website: www.epa.gov/climatechange

The website of the EPA's Climate Change Division offers comprehensive information on the issue of climate change in a way that is accessible and meaningful to all parts of society— communities, individuals, businesses, states, municipalities, and governments. The site offers a range of information on policies, science, health, and environmental effects, and action individuals can take.

U.S. Global Change Research Program
1717 Pennsylvania Ave. NW, Suite 250
Washington, DC 20006
(202) 223-6262
fax: (202) 223-3065
e-mail: information@usgcrp.gov
website: www.globalchange.gov/

The U.S. Global Change Research Program was established by president George H.W. Bush in 1989 and was continued by Congress in the Global Change Research Act of 1990. The program supports research on issues related to natural and human-induced climate changes and the implications of climate change for society. The website contains information about the effects of climate change on the United States as well as other articles and materials.

Worldchanging
1301 First Ave., Suite 301
Seattle, WA 98101
e-mail: contact@worldchanging.com
website: www.worldchanging.com

Worldchanging is a nonprofit media organization composed of a global network of independent journalists, designers, and thinkers promoting the idea that the tools, models, and ideas for building a "bright green future" are available now. In particular, it examines the important environmental stories that it feels the mainstream media overlook.

World Wildlife Fund (WWF)
1250 Twenty-fourth St. NW, Washington, DC 20090-7180
(202) 293-4800
website: www.worldwildlife.org/

The WWF is one of the largest conservation organizations, with almost 5 million supporters in more than one hundred countries. WWF's mission is to stop the degradation of the planet's natural environment and to build a future in which humans live in harmony with nature. Its website contains a helpful section on climate change that provides much information about the problem, its impact, and possible solutions.

BIBLIOGRAPHY

Books

Greg Craven, *What's the Worst That Could Happen? A Rational Response to the Climate Change Debate*. New York: Penguin, 2009.

Laurie David and Cambria Gordon, *The Down-to-Earth Guide to Global Warming*. New York: Orchard, 2007.

Tim Flannery, *Now or Never: Why We Must Act Now to End Climate Change and Create a Sustainable Future*. New York: Atlantic Monthly Press, 2009.

————, *We Are the Weather Makers: The History of Climate Change*. Somerville, MA: Candlewick, 2009.

Howard Friel, *The Lomborg Deception: Setting the Record Straight About Global Warming*. New Haven, CT: Yale University Press, 2010.

Al Gore, *An Inconvenient Truth: The Crisis of Global Warming*. New York: Viking, 2007.

Christopher C. Homer, *The Politically Incorrect Guide to Global Warming and Environmentalism*. Washington, DC: Regnery, 2007.

Thomas R. Karl, Jerry M. Melillo, and Thomas C. Peterson, eds., *Global Climate Change Impacts in the United States*. New York: Cambridge University Press, 2009. (Also available online at www.globalchange.gov/usimpacts.)

Elizabeth Kolbert, *Field Notes from a Catastrophe: Man, Nature, and Climate Change*. London: Bloomsbury, 2006.

Barbara A. Lewis, *The Teen Guide to Global Action: How to Connect with Others (Near & Far) to Create Social Change*. Minneapolis: Free Spirit, 2007.

Bjørn Lomborg, *Cool It: The Skeptical Environmentalist's Guide to Global Warming*. New York: Knopf, 2007.

James Lovelock, *The Vanishing Face of Gaia: A Final Warning*. New York: Basic Books, 2009.

Bill McKibben, *Earth: Making a Life on a Tough New Planet*. New York: Times Books, 2010.

Chris Mooney, *Storm World: Hurricanes, Politics, and the Battle over Global Warming*. Orlando, FL: Harcourt, 2007.

David de Rothschild, *The Live Earth Global Warming Survival Handbook: 77 Essential Skills to Stop Climate Change*. Emmaus, PA: Rodale, 2008.

Jenn Savedge, *The Green Teen: The Eco-friendly Teen's Guide to Saving the Planet*. Gabriola Island, BC: New Society, 2009.

Jerry Silver, *Global Warming and Climate Change Demystified: A Self-Teaching Guide*. New York: McGraw-Hill, 2008.

S. Fred Singer, *Unstoppable Global Warming: Every 1,500 Years*. Lanham, MD: Rowman & Littlefield, 2007.

Linda Sivertson, *Generation Green: The Ultimate Teen Guide to Living an Eco-Friendly Life*. New York: Simon Pulse, 2008.

Alex Steffen, *Worldchanging: A User's Guide for the 21st Century*. New York: Abrams, 2006.

David Steinman, *Safe Trip to Eden: 10 Steps to Save Planet Earth from the Global Warming Meltdown*. New York: Thunder's Mouth, 2007.

William Sweet, *Kicking the Carbon Habit: Global Warming and the Case for Renewable and Nuclear Energy*. New York: Columbia University Press, 2006.

Peter Douglas Ward, *Under a Green Sky: Global Warming, the Mass Extinctions of the Past, and What They Mean for Our Future*. New York: Smithsonian, 2007.

Periodicals and Internet Sources

Jessica Camille Aguirre, "As Glaciers Melt, Bolivia Fights for the Good Life," *YES! Magazine*, March 22, 2010. www.yes magazine.org/planet/as-glaciers-melt-bolivia-fights-for-the-good-life.

Decca Aitkenhead, "'Enjoy Life While You Can,'" *Guardian* (Manchester, UK), March 1, 2008.

Tom Athanasiou, "Forward from Copenhagen: The Emissions Emergency Is a Crisis of Justice," *Earth Island Journal*, Spring 2010.

Sharon Begley, "We Can't Get There from Here," *Newsweek*, March 23, 2009.

Molly Bentley, "Guns and Sunshades to Rescue Climate," BBC News, March 2, 2006. http://news.bbc.co.uk/2/hi/science/nature/4762720.stm.

Stuart Clark, "What's Wrong with the Sun?" *New Scientist*, June 12, 2010.

Tim Dickinson, "The Climate Killers: Meet the 17 Polluters and Deniers Who Are Derailing Efforts to Curb Global Warming," *Rolling Stone*, January 21, 2010.

Gregg Easterbrook, "Global Warming: Who Loses—and Who Wins?" *Atlantic Monthly*, April 2007.

The Economist, "The Science of Climate Change: The Clouds of Unknowing," March 20, 2010.

Erika Engelhaupt, "Engineering a Cooler Earth: Researchers Brainstorm Radical Ways to Counter Climate Change," *Science News*, June 5, 2010.

McKenzie Funk, "Capitalists of Chaos: Who's Cashing In on Global Warming?" *Rolling Stone*, May 27, 2010.

Jeff Goodell, "As the World Burns: How Big Oil and Big Coal Mounted One of the Most Aggressive Lobbying Campaigns in History to Block Progress on Global Warming," *Rolling Stone*, January 21, 2010.

Fred Guterl, "Will Climate Go Over the Edge?" *Newsweek International*, March 2, 2009.

Johann Hari, "The Wrong Kind of Green," *Nation*, March 22, 2010.

Michael T. Klare, "Avatar: The Prequel," TomDispatch, February 23, 2010. www.tomdispatch.com/post/175210/tomgram%3A_michael_klare%2C_another_planet_or_james_cameron/#more.

Jon A. Krosnick, "The Climate Majority," *New York Times*, June 9, 2010.

Jonathan Leake and Chris Hastings, "World Misled over Himalayan Glacier Meltdown," *Sunday Times* (London), January 17, 2010. www.timesonline.co.uk/tol/news/environment/article6991177.ece.

Rachel Morris, "To the Lifeboats: What Happens When Your Country Drowns? Meet the Coming Tide of Climate Refugees," *Mother Jones*, November/December 2009.

Naomi Oreskes and Erik Conway, "Global Warming Deniers and Their Proven Strategy of Doubt," *Yale Environment 360*, June 10, 2010. http://e360.yale.edu/content/feature.msp?id=2285.

Bob Reiss, "Barrow, Alaska: Ground Zero for Climate Change," *Smithsonian*, March 2010. www.smithsonianmag.com/science-nature/Barrow-Alaska-Ground-Zero-for-Climate-Change.html.

Jim Robbins, "What's Killing the Great Forests of the American West?" *Yale Environment 360*, March 15, 2010. http://e360.yale.edu/content/feature.msp?id=2252.

Ross Robertson, "A Brighter Shade of Green," *What Is Enlightenment?* October/December 2007. www.enlightennext.org/magazine/j38/j38.asp.

Alan Robock, "20 Reasons Why Geoengineering May Be a Bad Idea," *Bulletin of the Atomic Scientists*, May/June 2008.

Rebecca Solnit, "350 Degrees of Inseparability: The Good News About the Very Bad News (About Climate Change),"

CommonDreams, April 22, 2010. www.commondreams.org/view/2010/04/22-9.

Alex Steffen, "Counterpoint: Dangers of Focusing Solely on Climate Change," *Wired*, May 19, 2008. www.wired.com/science/planetearth/magazine/16-06/sb_carbon.

———, "Seeing Past the BP Spill," Worldchanging, June 16, 2010. www.worldchanging.com/archives/011286.html.

Doug Struck, "Buying Carbon Offsets May Ease Eco-guilt but Not Global Warming," *Christian Science Monitor*, April 20, 2010. www.csmonitor.com/Environment/2010/0420/Buying-carbon-offsets-may-ease-eco-guilt-but-not-global-warming.

Audrey Webb, "The Division over Multiplication," *Earth Island Journal*, Summer 2009.

Graeme Wood, "Re-engineering the Earth," *Atlantic*, June 2, 2009.

INDEX

PICTURE CREDITS

© Ace Stock Limited/Alamy Images, 28

AP Images, 6, 11, 22, 31, 39, 44, 86

Cengage Learning/Gale, 14, 20, 33, 37, 47, 53, 61, 67, 82

Richard R. Hansen/Photo Researchers, Inc., 77

Yves Herman/Reuters/Landov, 54

Jon Pelling/PA Photos/Landov, 58

Barbara L. Salisbury/The Washington Times/Landov, 72

Victor Habbick Visions/Photo Researchers, Inc., 64